THE SONG

 SING IT.

Sing it and say it, can anyone play it?
There's no need to be shy.
Sing it and say it, can anyone play it?
Come on, let's give it a try.

You'll soon learn the tune in a jiff and a half,
You'll soon learn the words, they might make you laugh!

So listen to me, there's no need to read,
Rhyme and rhythm are all you need –

 SAY IT.

Sing it with me on the count of three –
One, two, three, four!

 SING IT.

Sing it and say it, can anyone play it?
There's no need to be shy.
Sing it and say it, can anyone play it?
Come on, let's give it a try.

MUSICAL SCORE – page 21

ARE WE THERE YET?

A grin-inducing number to set us off on our journey. Stand by for sympathy from parents!

 SING IT. Allocate the lines as we've suggested or to suit the vocal talents of your class.

 ART & CRAFT. A touch of the 'Blue Peters' could be handy here for making a car from cardboard boxes, washing-up liquid bottles and some sticky-backed plastic! Alright, alright, use five chairs then.

 DRAMA. Hold auditions for Mum's role. Let the class vote. Have the riot police standing by. The child who can wag her finger the loudest usually wins. Dad has a non-speaking, but quietly humming role. The three children could be bright, argumentative types. Well, at least that way, all the trouble is in one place.

 DRAMA. 1st verse: Dad's driving. Mum's in the passenger seat – and in the back . . . three little horrors – er, sorry, children.

Chorus: Barely out of the drive and they've started the questions. **ARE WE THERE YET?** is giving Mum high blood pressure.

 TOPIC. 2nd verse: Travel project time. Send the class out with Mums and Dads on Saturday to gather free holiday brochures. Let's collate a collage. Wall charts, then. How long are the different journeys? How deep beneath the sea is the Tunnel? Who invented the hovercraft and how does it work? Who's been on a ferry? Where was the car stored during the journey? What did the sea feel like? What sounds and smells did you notice? Which port did you depart from?

 DRAMA. Chorus: Nearly time for Mum's nervous breakdown. Dad's stopped humming and taken up whistling.

 TOPIC. 3rd verse: Practice Bonjour, mon père, ma mère. Add Grandmère and Grandpère.

 TOPIC. They're travelling south to see the sun. How hot will it be in the south of France in the summer holidays? Which crops grow there? Maps and wallcharts to the fore again, folks!

 PLAY IT. Percussion accompaniment – see Musical Score (page 23).

Sing it and Say it
A BOOKFUL of FRANCE
by SARA RIDGLEY and GAVIN MOLE

CONTENTS

Note to Producer
Writers and Publishers receive royalties through performances of their works as well as the sale of sheet music. If these works are to be performed as musicals, then a licence will be required. Applications should be made in writing to The Copyright Department, International Music Publications Limited, Southend Road, Woodford Green, Essex IG8 8HN. Please state the title of the work and the proposed dates of performance.

Series Editor: Mark Mumford

Music arranged and processed by Barnes Music Engraving Ltd
East Sussex TN22 4HA, England

Cover Design by Paul Clark Designs

Published 1995

© International Music Publications Limited
Southend Road, Woodford Green, Essex IG8 8HN, England

INTRODUCTION

Welcome to **SING IT AND SAY IT (can anyone play it?)** and to a new way of learning, teaching and having fun!

Each **SING IT AND SAY IT** collection concentrates on a specific subject and offers a variety of songs that can be performed as individual pieces, combined to make three ten-minute mini-musicals or linked together to create a thirty-minute show.

To allow for easy and practical teaching, the book has been divided into three sections, clearly identifying each mini-musical. Director's Notes and song lyrics for each section are grouped together. They come first each time, followed by the complete musical score for the section. This makes continuous playing easier when performing your mini-musical.

The songs are packed with lively lyrics, guaranteed to appeal to the children of today. They are easy to teach and fun to learn with music that is catchy, memorable and full of character.

The Director's Notes are a complete 'selection box' of suggestions. They will help to add a real cross-curricular flavour to activities and performances. Drama, instrumental accompaniments, sound effects and topic ideas will all combine to make a complete stage performance packed with learning and laughter.

Throughout the book we've used the following symbols and titles to help you find your way around:

 SING IT.   **DRAMA.**   **ARTS & CRAFTS.**

 SAY IT.   **SOUND EFFECTS. (FX.)**   **TOPICS ARISING.**

 PLAY IT.

SING IT AND SAY IT has been created by Sara and Gavin to bring entertainment into education and therefore it has been written for both children and teachers. Enjoy it!

ACKNOWLEDGEMENTS
Heartfelt thanks to Cheron Mole (tolerance, support, musical skill, endless coffee, great lunches), Joyce and Ed Woodwark (financial help, boundless enthusiasm), Caroline Coxon (French tips) and Andy Spiller (inspiration in the recording studio).

Look out for other titles in the **SING IT AND SAY IT** series. Check with your local dealer for details.

1 LET'S MEET MAURICE

CONTENTS

This **SING IT AND SAY IT** episode takes us on a musical journey over the Channel and round the north of France with our young guide, Maurice.

We encounter several of Maurice's friends, learn some French, discover a few historical facts and above all, have plenty of fun. Allez! Allez!

SING IT AND SAY IT

DIRECTOR'S NOTES

Our first song expresses the essence of the **SING IT AND SAY IT** project:

SING IT.   Singing easy-to-learn music
SAY IT.   Saying entertaining words with rhyme and rhythm
PLAY IT.   Playing simple accompaniments

We'd add **BUILDING** to that list. Building confidence, vocabulary and musical ability. Building concentration and timing, teamwork and, that elusive quality, discipline!

The other term which encapsulates **SING IT AND SAY IT** is FUN. Fun in learning *and* fun in teaching

 SING IT.   The first and last sections of this song are identical for easy learning and, (with a small change to the last section), the whole song is repeated at the end of this 10-minute episode.

 SING IT.   **SING IT AND SAY IT** can be performed as an ensemble, in separate groups or as a solo.

 FX.   Clapping and clicking of fingers will find their natural places in this song.

 DRAMA.   However you use the material, your class will have plenty of suggestions for actions and simple dance routines. Someone will want to be the conductor and everyone will want to shout "Four!" (after One, Two, Three). Let them, they're learning!

THE SONG

 SING IT.

1st CHILD:	We're taking a trip across the sea,
2nd CHILD:	We're going to France on holiday,
3rd CHILD:	We're travelling south to see the sun,
1st CHILD:	It's the longest journey our Mum's ever done.

1st CHILD:	Are we there yet, Mum?
MUM:	Not yet.
2nd CHILD:	Is it far now, Mum?
MUM:	Not far.
3rd CHILD:	How much longer, Mum?
MUM:	Not long.
1st CHILD:	When will . . .?
MUM:	If you keep on asking, then your Dad will stop the car!

1st CHILD:	We could sail on a ferry or fly on a plane,
2nd CHILD:	Or go through the tunnel, le Shuttle's the train.
3rd CHILD:	The hovercraft flies, the hovercraft floats,
1st CHILD:	Mum says it's an aeroplane crossed with a boat.

1st CHILD:	Are we there yet, Mum?
MUM:	Not yet.
2nd CHILD:	Is it far now, Mum?
MUM:	Not far.
3rd CHILD:	How much longer, Mum?
MUM:	Not long.
1st CHILD:	When will . . .?
MUM:	If you keep on moaning, then we won't come here again!

1st CHILD:	We've all learnt our French so we can say
2nd CHILD:	Bonjour, bonjour now we're away
3rd CHILD:	And I can say Dad, mon père, mon père
1st CHILD:	And Mum's la mère

MUSICAL SCORE – page 23

LET'S MEET MAURICE

DIRECTOR'S NOTES

Here he is, our guide for this **SING IT AND SAY IT** journey. Maurice has his own theme music which appears in your ears every time he shows his little face.

 DRAMA. Maurice is about 7 years old, a miniature gentleman. No, we know you won't have one of those in your class, but pick the one with the most acting ability, draw a pencil-thin Gallic moustache on him (or her) and ooh là là! A trainee heart-throb à la Monsieur Chevalier.

 DRAMA. He may have a 'signature' action – perhaps a sweeping bow or (and now we're being really malicious), Maurice may love to kiss the hand of a lady . . . No, don't tear the book up – it gets better.

 DRAMA. Now, Maurice is proud of his country and is looking forward to introducing his new English friends to France. I know that's a hard-to-digest concept, but do your best.

 TOPIC. Good opportunity to learn 'Bienvenu' for 'Welcome!' and do a 'Je m'appelle' run round the class with each child adding the closest French version of their name.

 DRAMA. 'Ma belle France', 'Venez à Paris' and 'Maintenant' can all be accompanied by a classful of Gallic shrugs and expressive hand movements.

 TOPIC. And, just in case you thought we'd forgotten, it's back to the map for pointing out Paris.

 DRAMA. Simple dancing or swaying moves will appear during this short piece to be revived when we next meet Maurice before **METRO MAX**.

Bonne chance!

THE SONG

 SAY IT.   MAURICE: And the sea is la mer!

 SAY IT.   1st CHILD: Who are you?

 SING IT.   MAURICE: Bienvenu! I welcome you.
Je m'appelle Maurice.
I'm here to show you
Ma belle France,
Venez à Paris.

We learn some words,
We find some friends,
We hear some history too.

Je m'appelle Maurice,
Bienvenu!
Je m'appelle Maurice,
I welcome you!

 SAY IT.   Et maintenant, some words!

MUSICAL SCORE – page 28

CONFUSED?

DIRECTOR'S NOTES

 SING IT. This is fast and furious. Maurice is trying to teach his new friends some French but he learns as much as he teaches here. Well, that's the idea, anyway.

 ART & CRAFT. Class activity beforehand should include drawings or paintings of:

a pair of hands
a man
an ice cream
a glass of milk
a French baguette
a pen
an egg

 DRAMA. You could use real ice-cream, real milk and a real egg, but don't blame us for the melée. A real French baguette and a real pen may not be so messy, but could be equally dangerous as Maurice and his English friend could certainly use them in a duel during the song – it's up to you! Just make sure your school has adequate insurance cover.

 TOPIC. What other words exist to confuse us in French and English? No, you tell us, class.

THE SONG

 SING IT.

MAURICE:	Voici les mains.
1st CHILD:	No, that's a man.
MAURICE:	Mais oui, les mains.
1st CHILD:	No, that is a man.
MAURICE:	Mains!
1st CHILD:	Man!
MAURICE:	Mains!
1st CHILD:	Man!
BOTH:	Mains/Man!
MAURICE: (together)	Tu ne me comprends pas? Ce sont des mains.
1st CHILD:	Don't you understand me? That's a man.

MAURICE:	Voici la glace.
1st CHILD:	No, that's an ice cream.
MAURICE:	Mais oui, la glace.
1st CHILD:	No, this is a glass.
MAURICE:	Glace!
1st CHILD:	Glass!
MAURICE:	Glace!
1st CHILD:	Glass!
BOTH:	Glace/Glass!
MAURICE: (together)	Tu ne me comprends pas? C'est la glace.
1st CHILD:	Don't you understand me? That's ice cream.

MAURICE:	C'est un verre, un verre de lait.
1st CHILD:	Un verre de lait?
MAURICE:	Un verre de lait.
1st CHILD:	Lait is milk and glass is verre.
MAURICE:	Mais oui! C'est ça!
1st CHILD:	I think we're there!
MAURICE:	Et voici du pain.
1st CHILD:	No, this is a pen.
MAURICE:	C'est un stylo.
1st CHILD:	He's right, you know.
MAURICE:	Et voici un oeuf.
1st CHILD:	You're right, it's enough!
MAURICE:	Un oeuf!
1st CHILD:	Enough!
MAURICE:	Un oeuf!
1st CHILD:	Enough!
BOTH:	ENOUGH!!
MAURICE:	Now you understand me?
1st CHILD:	Je comprends!

MUSICAL SCORE – page 29

TO PARIS WITH MAURICE

Here comes Maurice's music again!

TOPIC. Our journey takes us on to the capital. Plenty of opportunity to discuss the Sacré Coeur, the Bois de Boulogne, Arc de Triomphe, Tomb of the Unknown Soldier etc.

ART & CRAFT. Drawings/paintings/models of famous Paris landmarks are a must. How about the Arc de Triomphe built from recycled toothpaste tubes and lolly sticks? Break out the Gloy.

Stand by to meet Maurice's friends, they're quite something!

THE SONG

SING IT.   MAURICE: So here we are,
Nous arrivons –
Beautiful Paris!

Such sights to see,
Such history –
Our première city.

SAY IT.   Et maintenant, some friends!

MUSICAL SCORE – page 33

METRO MAX

DRAMA. How's this for an idea? **METRO MAX**, King of the Tracks, bursts through a hoop of paper and stuns the audience! Oh, shame. Never mind, we're sure you'll think of an equally dramatic entrance for this character. **METRO MAX** may wear a beret and Rayban sunglasses as befitting the cool tube he is. Your class will have other ideas – that's the plan.

DRAMA. Hey, how about this! It's even better than the paper hoop idea. Why not put **METRO MAX** on roller skates? Why not put all his carriages on roller skates? Great! (Excuse me a second, who's on the phone? Sir Andrew Lloyd-Who?!)

ART & CRAFT. I bet you wish you'd never started this. Enlist a painting-minded parent (after all, they're usually free of charge) and get them to organise your class to design a muriel – sorry, mourul – er, a wall-painting of a cutaway subterranean tunnel with views of the Paris skyline above. Cafés, Notre Dame, the Champs Elysées etc in silhouette against a night sky, a sunny sky and in a storm. The perfect set for **METRO MAX**.

FX. METRO MAX is held in legendary esteem by his passengers and carriages so a little respectful whispering wouldn't come amiss when his name is spoken or sung. Tricky thing, respect. See what you can do. Clapping or finger-clicking supplement this song, too.

 TOPIC. Take a look at the Metro map and compare it to the London Underground for a historical/geographical project. Ask the class to imagine how tunnels were built under the River Seine – and how they would persuade the first passengers to 'go underground like a mole'.

| THE SONG |

 SAY IT. Metro Max! Metro Max! Metro Max! Metro Max!

 SING IT. He's a smooth operator, he works in the dark,
Gliding along under Paris's parks
And Paris's pavements and pavement cafés,
Underneath Notre Dame and the Champs Elysées.

 SAY IT. Metro Max! Metro Max!

 SING IT. Metro Max! King of the Tracks!
Feel so fine, see him sparkle and shine.
Right on time all the way down the line
'Cos he's Metro Max, King of the Tracks!

 SAY IT. Metro Max! Metro Max!

 SING IT. He's a smooth operator, he works day and night,
Underground like a mole, never seeing the light.
Never seeing the sun, never seeing the rain,
Underneath the Sorbonne and the great River Seine.

 SAY IT. Metro Max! Metro Max!

 SING IT. Metro Max! King of the Tracks!
Feel so fine, see him sparkle and shine.
Right on time all the way down the line
'Cos he's Metro Max, King of the Tracks,
Metro Max, King of the Tracks,

 SAY IT. Metro Max, King of the Tracks!

| MUSICAL SCORE – page 34 |

THE EIFFEL TOWER

| DIRECTOR'S NOTES |

 DRAMA. Building an **EIFFEL TOWER** out of children could be fun. No, really. Your choice. This song needs a character who can manage a French accent if possible. Not compulsory.

 DRAMA. Non-Eiffels could be usefully employed as barges and boats chugging past on the Seine waving or chatting to our friend, the Tower.

 ART & CRAFT. Others could hold up sun-painted placards. Rain, we leave to your imagination.

 TOPIC. Ideal for historical topic work is **EIFFEL**. The French Revolution, Bastille Day and all that, you know. He was due to be destroyed in the early part of the century (listen to us, calling him 'he' – anyone would think he was real!), but he was so handy as a transmitter mast during World War I that he won a reprieve, bless him.

 TOPIC. More 'Eiffel-facts' to appeal to your French-minded pupils could include info on Gustave Eiffel; how high is **EIFFEL** (321m); what does he weigh (9700 tons); how far he sways in a high wind (no, we don't know either). What can you see from the top and how many steps and stages are there?

 DRAMA. The mention of the metro could lead to a brief cameo by **METRO MAX** whose ego is probably huge enough to handle it by now – it's up to you.

 TOPIC. More history with Edward VII (as in 'Queen Victoria died, I knew her son').

 SING IT. Plenty of opportunity for a backing chorus here with the 'oooh, aaah' factor. Lots of repetition and echoes to play with.

 FX. Good for clapping and stamping, clicking their fingers or tapping their toes under **EIFFEL**'s spoken section.

THE SONG

 SING IT.

EIFFEL: I've stood here for years like a four-legged stork,
CHORUS: Like a four-legged stork
EIFFEL: And sometimes I'm tempted to go for a walk,
CHORUS: Go for a walk.
EIFFEL: I chat to the barges and boats on the Seine,
I suffer in sunshine and revel in rain.

EIFFEL: Don't take me away!
CHORUS: Don't take him away!
EIFFEL: Don't take me away!
CHORUS: Don't take him away!
EIFFEL: They wanted to take me away,
CHORUS: Oooh, aaah!
EIFFEL: Oh, please let me stay!
CHORUS: Oh, please let him stay!
EIFFEL: Oh, please let me stay!
CHORUS: Oh, please let him stay!
EIFFEL: Et voilà! They did let me stay.

 SAY IT.

EIFFEL: Bonjour! My name is Eiffel. Alors, I'm in charge of Paris. You see, when I was built for the World Exhibition in 1889, not everybody liked me, but I was far too useful, so voilà! They did let me stay.

 SING IT.

EIFFEL: Then they opened the Metro when I was just ten,
CHORUS: When he was just ten.
EIFFEL: The trains underground have been running since then,
CHORUS: Running since then.
EIFFEL: And over the Channel in 1901,
Queen Victoria died – I knew her son.

EIFFEL: Don't take me away!
CHORUS: Don't take him away!
EIFFEL: Don't take me away!
CHORUS: Don't take him away!
EIFFEL: They wanted to take me away,
CHORUS: Oooh, aaah!
EIFFEL: Oh, please let me stay!
CHORUS: Oh, please let him stay!
EIFFEL: Oh, please let me stay!
CHORUS: Oh, please let him stay!
EIFFEL: Et voilà! They did let me stay!

MUSICAL SCORE – page 36

THE DRAGON OF FINISTERE

DIRECTOR'S NOTES

We're back to the coast now near the end of our whistle-stop French tour in this 10-minute episode.

 TOPIC. Finistere (literally 'End of the Earth' – you knew that already), that rocky outcrop on the north-west corner of Brittany (map attack), has been notorious since the days of the Phoenician tin traders (c.330 BC) as a graveyard for many a proud sailing ship (but you knew that, too).

 TOPIC. Pounded by Atlantic breakers and the moods of the English Channel (more map), Finistere has a LEGEND! A mythical dragon lives in a cave under the waves and eats boats for breakfast. (He doesn't really. I think . . .)

 SAY IT. Use 5 pairs of children for this piece – or give 10 individuals a line each and build up the pace until 'giant teeth!' – then stop frightening them. No, stop it.

 ART & CRAFT. Dragon painting / drawing / pottery / model-making extends the project. Name that dragon in one. Could be a girl dragon? French or English? Maybe he or she defected from Devon or came over from Cornwall? (More map work plus feature on Celts and Bretons?)

 ART & CRAFT. Got any old green sheets or curtains? How about a Chinese New Year-style dragon costume with four children inside? (See **SING IT AND SAY IT** Festivals Around The World – also from IMP – for more information on this topic). Crepe paper and egg boxes can work wonders with such artistic projects. So can a voluntary art-minded parent.

 ART & CRAFT. Organise a galleon-painting hour (more history). Ships on placards 'walked' across are very effective.

 PLAY IT. Percussion accompaniment – see Musical Score (page 39).

Good luck, me hearties!

THE SONG

 SAY IT.

1st PAIR: Off the coast of Finistere,
Lies a dragon in his lair.

2nd PAIR: (slightly faster)   Hungry in his lair he hides,
Hiding from the turning tides.

3rd PAIR: (faster)   Turning tides reveal the beach,
Ships sail further out of reach.

4th PAIR: (Panicky)   Out of reach they might escape,
Escape the dragon's hungry gape.

5th PAIR: (frightened)   Hungry gape of giant teeth!
                  (relieved)   Giant teeth? No, just a reef.

MUSICAL SCORE – page 39

COASTS AND OCEANS

DIRECTOR'S NOTES

Heart-rate returned to normal after **THE DRAGON OF FINISTERE**?

 TOPIC.   Our cast are now standing gingerly on the rocks looking out over the Atlantic on one side, with America over the horizon and the English Channel on the other. Map time, chaps.

 SING IT or **SAY IT**.   **COASTS AND OCEANS** can be spoken or sung with humming or our old friend, 'aaah-ing', under the words.

 ART & CRAFT.   Another chance to use the collage you made for **ARE WE THERE YET?** You DID make a collage for **ARE WE THERE YET?**, didn't you? And yes, we are nearly there. At the end of this episode, that is.

THE SONG

 SING IT.

> If you gaze across the ocean
> From the western coast of France,
> You'll see rolling, rolling breakers
> In a never-ending dance.
> On a stormy day, it's frantic.
> Feel the force of the Atlantic
> Sending winds and waves and weather
> From America to France.

> If you gaze across the ocean
> From the northern coast of France,
> You'll see busy, busy ferries
> In a never-ending dance.
> Far below them is the Tunnel
> Underneath the English Channel
> Sending winds and waves and weather
> From the English hills to France.

MUSICAL SCORE – page 41

AU REVOIR FROM MAURICE

DRAMA.   Time to bid farewell to our guide. Should he kiss all the girls on both cheeks, do you suppose? It would have the Mums weeping in the aisles, but if you feel blood would be shed, perhaps he should just wave!

THE SONG

SING IT.

MAURICE: Et maintenant, it's time for me to say
Au revoir to you.
I hope you will remember me,
I will remember you.

We learnt some words,
We found some friends,
We heard some history too.

Je m'appelle Maurice, au revoir to you.
Je m'appelle Maurice, bye-bye to you!

MUSICAL SCORE – page 42

SING IT AND SAY IT (Finale)

 SING IT. We're good to you, aren't we? Not a lot of extra work involved here, we promise. You and your class already know the words for the closing number because it was also the opening number. Now, come along, it was only ten minutes ago!

 SING IT. An option to replace One, Two, Three – Four! with Un, Deux, Trois – Quatre! if you feel like a final French flavour.

 DRAMA. The repeat of the last line creates a rousing finish. We suggest a pantomime-style deep bow or similar theatrical flourish at this point before the audience storms the stage for autographs!

 TOPIC. Organise your class to write 30 words each, giving their impressions of this **SING IT AND SAY IT** episode. It's a very useful exercise and we always find the results fascinating. If you'd like to pass on their insights and comments to us, we'd be delighted to hear from you – and your class.

THE SONG

 SING IT. Sing it and say it, can anyone play it?
There's no need to be shy.
Sing it and say it, can anyone play it?
Come on, let's give it a try.

You'll soon learn the tune in a jiff and a half,
You'll soon learn the words, they might make you laugh!

So listen to me, there's no need to read,
Rhyme and rhythm are all you need –

 SAY IT. Sing it with me on the count of three –
One, two, three, four!

 SING IT. Sing it and say it, can anyone play it?
There's no need to be shy.
Sing it and say it, can anyone play it?
Come on, let's give it a,
Let's give it a,
Let's give it a try!

MUSICAL SCORE – page 43

LET'S MEET MAURICE

SING IT AND SAY IT

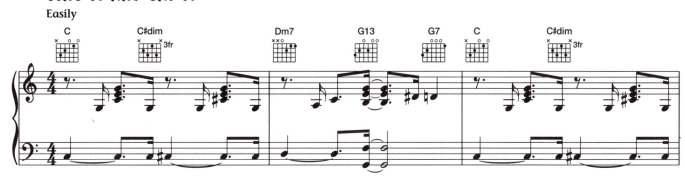

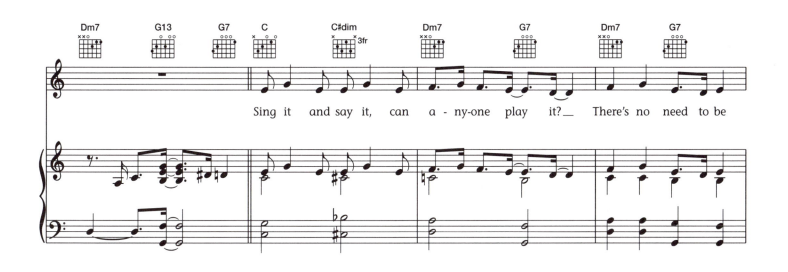

Sing it and say it, can a-ny-one play it?__ There's no need to be

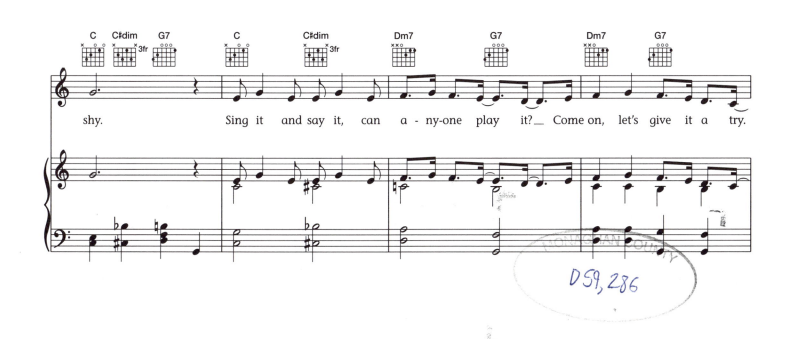

shy. Sing it and say it, can a-ny-one play it?__ Come on, let's give it a try.

Sing it and say it, can a-ny-one play it?__ Come on, let's give it a try!

ARE WE THERE YET?

Holiday tempo

1st CHILD

We're

CAR HORN

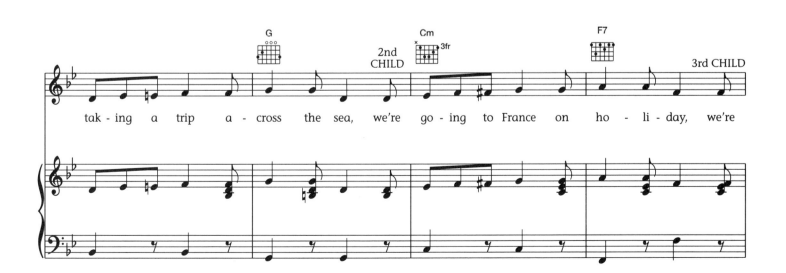

tak-ing a trip a-cross the sea, we're go-ing to France on ho-li-day, we're

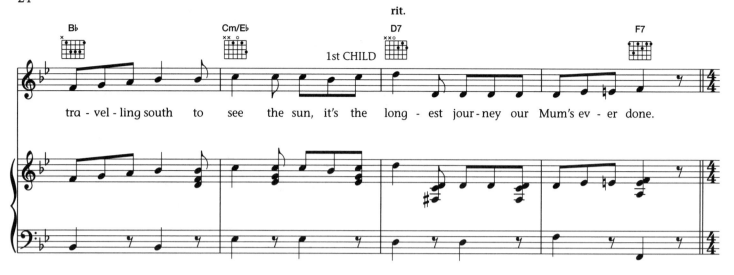

tra - vel - ling south to see the sun, it's the long - est jour - ney our Mum's ev - er done.

Bored tempo

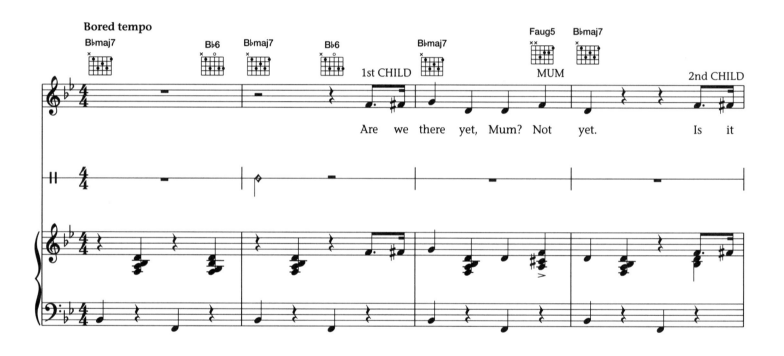

Are we there yet, Mum? Not yet. Is it

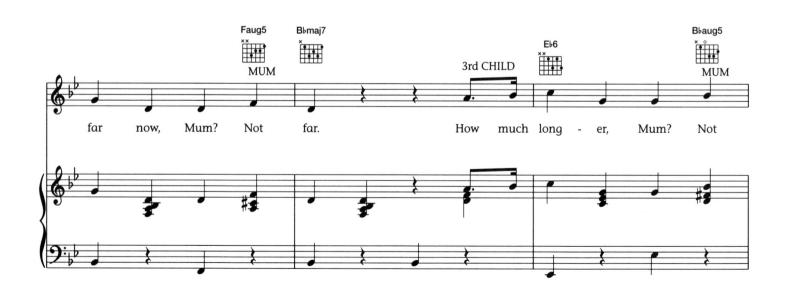

far now, Mum? Not far. How much long - er, Mum? Not

long. When will...? If you keep on ask - ing, then your Dad will stop the car!

Holiday tempo

We could sail on a fer - ry or fly on a plane, or

go through the Tun - nel, le Shut - tle's the train. The ho - ver - craft flies, the

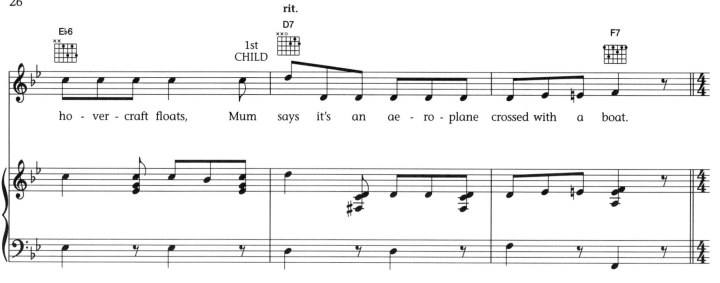

ho - ver - craft floats, Mum says it's an ae - ro - plane crossed with a boat.

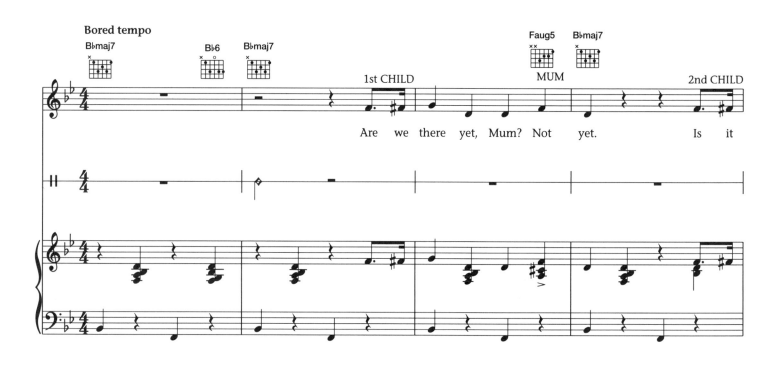

Are we there yet, Mum? Not yet. Is it

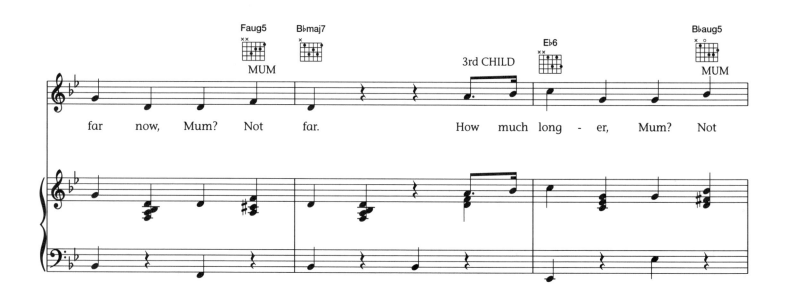

far now, Mum? Not far. How much long - er, Mum? Not

long. When will...? If you keep on moan - ing, then we won't come here a-gain!

We've all learnt our French so we can say bon -

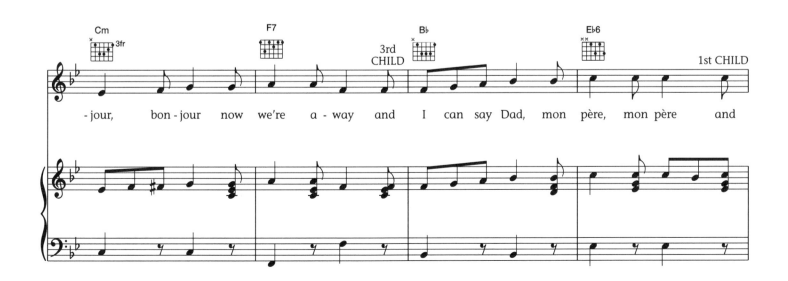

- jour, bon - jour now we're a - way and I can say Dad, mon père, mon père and

LET'S MEET MAURICE

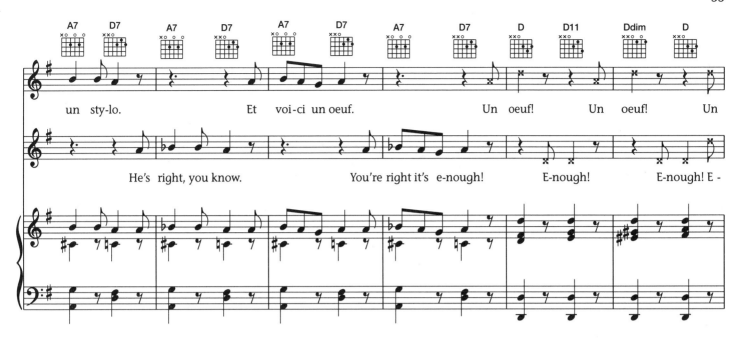

un sty-lo. Et voi-ci un oeuf. Un oeuf! Un oeuf! Un

He's right, you know. You're right it's e-nough! E-nough! E-nough! E-

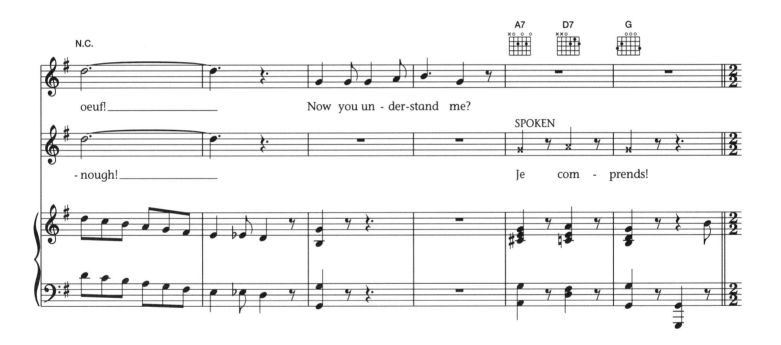

oeuf!_____ Now you un-der-stand me?

SPOKEN

-nough!_____ Je com - prends!

TO PARIS WITH MAURICE

Friendly tempo

MAURICE

So here we are, nous ar-ri-vons— beau-ti-ful Pa-

THE EIFFEL TOWER

In the style of a tall metal tower

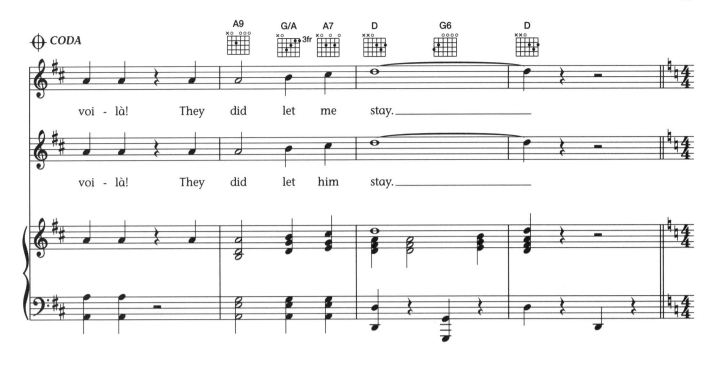

voi - là! They did let me stay._____

voi - là! They did let him stay._____

THE DRAGON OF FINISTERE

Slowly, gradually getting faster

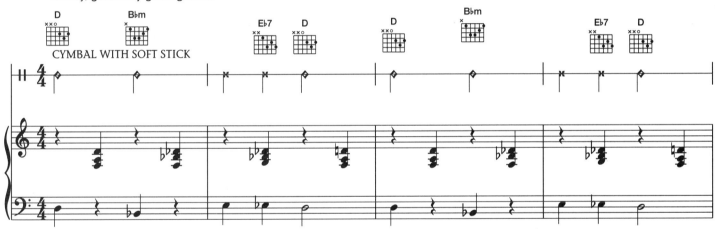

CYMBAL WITH SOFT STICK

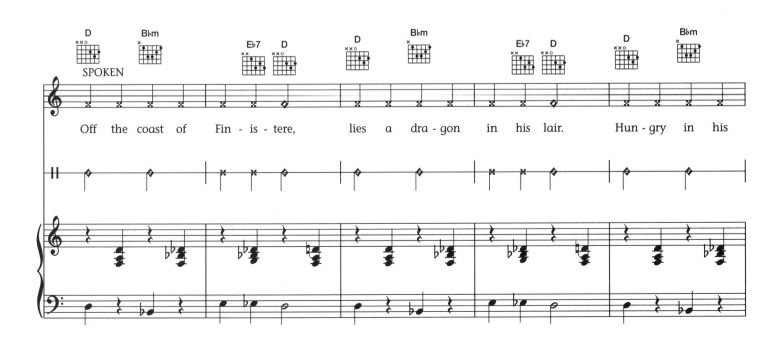

SPOKEN

Off the coast of Fin - is - tere, lies a dra - gon in his lair. Hun - gry in his

COASTS AND OCEANS

In the tempo of a light breeze

If you gaze a - cross the o - cean from the
gaze a - cross the o - cean from the

west - ern coast of France, you'll see roll - ing, roll - ing break - ers in a ne - ver - end - ing dance. On a
north - ern coast of France, you'll see bu - sy, bu - sy fer - ries in a ne - ver - end - ing dance. Far be -

stor - my day, it's fran - tic. Feel the force of the At - lan - tic send - ing winds and waves and
- low them is the Tun - nel un - der - neath the Eng - lish Chan - nel send - ing winds and waves and

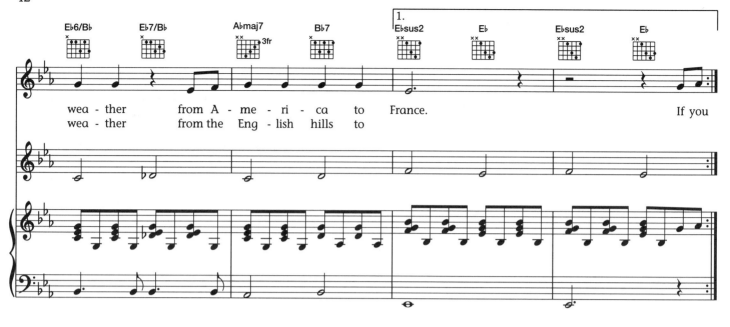

wea - ther   from A - me - ri - ca   to   France.   If you
wea - ther   from the Eng - lish   hills   to

AU REVOIR FROM MAURICE

Friendly tempo

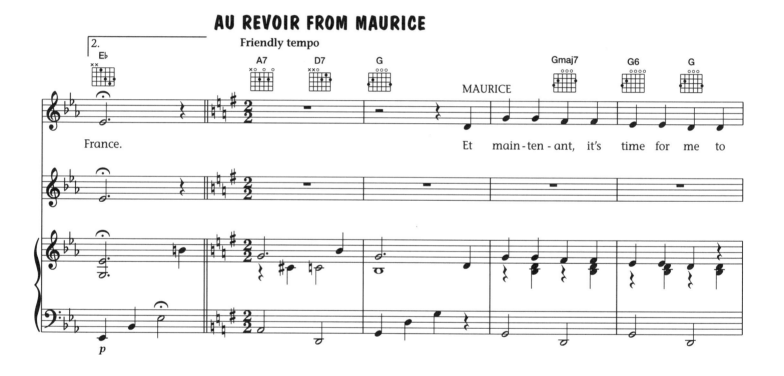

France.

MAURICE

Et main-ten-ant, it's   time for me to

say   au revoir to   you.   I   hope you will re - mem-ber me, I   will re-mem-ber   you.   We

learnt some words, we found some friends, we heard some his - tory too.

Je m'a - ppelle Mau - rice, au revoir to you.

Je m'a - ppelle Mau - rice, bye - bye to you!

SING IT AND SAY IT

Easily

2 FRANCE'S FOUR CORNERS

CONTENTS

This **SING IT AND SAY IT** episode takes us on a journey to the prehistoric cave paintings at Lascaux, in the Dordogne; along the River Seine with two barges, Brigitte and Bertrand; up into the mountains with Bernard, the bearded vulture, and finally, to the sunny south to meet Jean-Louis, a palm tree of renown.

Enjoy your travels. Send us a postcard!

SING IT AND SAY IT

DIRECTOR'S NOTES

Our first song expresses the essence of the **SING IT AND SAY IT** project:

SING IT. Singing easy-to-learn music
SAY IT. Saying entertaining words with rhyme and rhythm
PLAY IT. Playing simple accompaniments

We'd add **BUILDING** to that list. Building confidence, vocabulary and musical ability. Building concentration and timing, teamwork and, that elusive quality, discipline!

The other term which encapsulates **SING IT AND SAY IT** is FUN. Fun in learning *and* fun in teaching

 SING IT. The first and last sections of this song are identical for easy learning and, (with a small change to the last section), the whole song is repeated at the end of this 10-minute episode.

 SING IT. **SING IT AND SAY IT** can be performed as an ensemble, in separate groups or as a solo.

 FX. Clapping and clicking of fingers will find their natural places in this song.

 DRAMA. However you use the material, your class will have plenty of suggestions for actions and simple dance routines. Someone will want to be the conductor and everyone will want to shout 'Four!' (after One, Two, Three). Let them, they're learning!

THE SONG

 SING IT.
Sing it and say it, can anyone play it?
There's no need to be shy.
Sing it and say it, can anyone play it?
Come on, let's give it a try.

You'll soon learn the tune in a jiff and a half,
You'll soon learn the words, they might make you laugh!

So listen to me, there's no need to read,
Rhyme and rhythm are all you need –

 SAY IT.
Sing it with me on the count of three –
One, two, three, four!

 SING IT.
Sing it and say it, can anyone play it?
There's no need to be shy.
Sing it and say it, can anyone play it?
Come on, let's give it a try.

MUSICAL SCORE – page 57

THE WEST OF FRANCE

DIRECTOR'S NOTES

TOPIC. Back to the map, chaps. What other crops and industry does the west of France support? We haven't looked at the fishing industry, but we're not stopping you. All that wonderful seafood they serve in the restaurants along the coast . . .

TOPIC. A study of the wine-growing areas would be fun. Different labels, types of grapes, vineyards and vintages, harvests and production methods. Send them round the supermarket on a Saturday with Mum and Dad to research the labels in the racks.

THE SONG

SING IT.

In the west of France
There are hills and plains
Growing grapes, growing grain in a gentle rain
And a soft summer breeze someone sent from Spain.

MUSICAL SCORE – page 59

LASCAUX

DIRECTOR'S NOTES

DRAMA. Picture the scene. We envisage the original four boys who discovered the caves telling this story, but they are now elderly gentlemen. Possibly, they revert to childhood (i.e. pulling off grey wigs and masks) for the chorus? Over to you.

TOPIC. Plenty of opportunity for history projects here. We've squeezed as much fact into the lyrics as we could – we'll leave the rest to you.

ART & CRAFT. Art content would be fun with a competition to draw or paint the best mammoth or bison. And no, we won't take any responsibility if they deface the walls in the School Hall. Find your own cave. Sidetrack on to Picasso if you wish.

TOPIC. Dovetails neatly into a project on materials used in cave paintings. How did they manage for brushes, for instance? And how did they get their models to stand still? And did the art class have a Christmas party?

 PLAY IT. Percussion accompaniment – see Musical Score (page 60).

THE SONG

 SAY IT.
In the region of Dordogne,
There's a place they call Lascaux
With a prehistoric secret –
Shall we tell you how we know?

 SING IT.
The year was 1940
And the four of us were there.
Then our dog was really naughty,
Disappearing in thin air.
But the cavern where we found him
Was amazing and astounding,
Full of prehistoric paintings
In their secret, silent lair.

There were bison here, ibex there,
Mega mammoths everywhere,
Prehistoric monsters living long ago!
Running deer, hairy bear,
Charcoal creatures everywhere,
Prehistoric monsters living long ago!

Now these caves are near Les Eyzies
In the valley of Vézère.
Massive Mesolithic mammals
Simply make you stand and stare.
Picasso's predecessors
Had no canvas to impress us,
Just those prehistoric paintings
In their secret, silent lair.

There were bison here, ibex there,
Mega mammoths everywhere,
Prehistoric monsters living long ago!
Running deer, hairy bear,
Charcoal creatures everywhere,
Prehistoric monsters living long ago!

MUSICAL SCORE – page 60

THE NORTH OF FRANCE

DIRECTOR'S NOTES

 TOPIC. The Bayeux Tapestry, Channel ports, Paris, the Seine estuary and its wildlife, Rouen and Joan of Arc, Caen, Reims, Le Mans, Brittany, Versailles – there's plenty to look at in the North of France.

 TOPIC. Dig around for some of the interesting old legends about the River Seine, like the story of Rulph, his daughter Calixte and her beau, Raoul.

THE SONG

 SING IT.

> In the north of France,
> It's so cool and clean,
> Endless acres of orchards of apples green,
> Endless barges and boats on the River Seine.

MUSICAL SCORE – page 62

BARGES ON THE SEINE

DIRECTOR'S NOTES

 ART & CRAFT. Brigitte is a feminine, prettily decorated barge, houseboat to her artistic owner, Phillippe. (Good time to try canal-boat painting with the gang – small jugs or watering cans are effective.)

 FX. The Barge Chorus could be issued with bells, hooters and horns – if you can bear the thought of it.

 TOPIC. Bertrand is a big, old, slightly beaten-up barge carrying his cargo of coal along the Seine (map time).

 DRAMA. Brigitte and Bertrand greet each other and wave goodbye as they chug on past. Aaaah, the course of true love . . .

THE SONG

 SING IT.

BRIGITTE: Bonjour, bonjour to you!

I'm a barge on the Seine,
Je m'appelle Brigitte.
I'm home to an artist,
Il s'appelle Phillippe.
I'm painted with flowers,
So dainty and so sweet
And sometimes at sunset,
You may hear me speak.

Peep-peep, peep-peep, je suis Brigitte.

BARGE CHORUS: Living on the River Seine,
Hard at work all day.
Wait until the sun goes down,
Then we come out to play.

BRIGITTE: Peep-peep, peep-peep!

BERTRAND: Bong-bong, bong-bong!
Bonjour, to you!

I'm a barge on the Seine,
Je m'appelle Bertrand.
I'm home to a boatman,
Il s'appelle Legrand.
I'm carrying coal
From Paris to Rouen
And sometimes at sunset,
You may hear my song.

Bong-bong, bong-bong, je suis Bertrand.

BARGE CHORUS: Living on the River Seine,
Hard at work all day.
Wait until the sun goes down,
Then we come out to play.

MUSICAL SCORE – page 63

THE EAST OF FRANCE

 TOPIC. It's mountain time. The Vosges, the Jura, the Alps, Mont Blanc. And we're not going to tell you that it's Europe's highest mountain at 4807 metres (15,760 feet) because you knew that already.

 TOPIC. Plenty of wildlife to discuss. Eagles, bear, lynx, wild cat, ptarmigan, mountain hare and, of course, vultures.

 TOPIC. The majority of French schools close for a month in the winter and everyone goes 'en vacances' to 'faire du ski'. Sounds good to us!

 TOPIC. Start an investigation of France's eastern borders – from the top: Belgium, Luxembourg, Germany, Switzerland, Italy and Monaco. Why are we telling you this? The children should be telling you this. Yes, it's back to the map – again.

THE SONG

 SING IT.

In the east of France
Where the mountains rise,
There is snow on Mont Blanc, even in July
And the vultures are circling in azure skies.

MUSICAL SCORE – page 68

BERNARD

 TOPIC. Now, Bernard is a Lammergeier. No, nor did we, so we looked it up. A Lammergeier is a Bearded Vulture, resident of France's mountains and one of the country's rarest raptors. (Bird of prey, dear, bird of prey.) Lammergeiers stand 1 metre high in their stockinged feet (ideal opportunity for measuring the height of your charges to compare with Bernard – and for learning French numbers).

 DRAMA. Now find the child with the stringiest neck and the baldest head and voilà! you've cast your Bernard.

DRAMA. If you can find a child with a 3 metre wingspan, please call us. We believe Bernard may wear a fringed scarf round his bare vulture neck for his stage show. He may also jump off a low podium a few times if you have a First Aid Officer in the audience.

 PLAY IT. Percussion accompaniments – see Musical Score (page 69).

THE SONG

 SING IT.

BERNARD:	(confidingly)	My name is Bernard. I'm fearsomely, awesomely scary. To tell you the truth, Of these mountains, I'm terribly wary.
	(shrugging)	I have to be scary, you see, It's simply expected of me. It's a natural part of my culture.
	(sulkily)	'S'not my fault I'm a vulture.
		I'm alright at night, But not in the light. I can't stand the sight,
	(panicky)	It fills me with fright And try as I might –
	(terrified)	I HATE HEIGHTS!
	(sternly)	But if anyone asks, My name is Bernard And I'm fearsomely, awesomely scary!
		My name is Bernard.
	(shaking head)	As a vulture, I'm really not valid. I ought to pick bones,
	(confidingly)	But I'd rather have quiche and a salad.
	(resignedly)	I have to eat carrion, you see, It's simply expected of me. It's a natural part of my culture.
	(resentfully)	S'not my fault I'm a vulture.
		I'm alright at night, But not in the light.
	(panicky)	I can't stand the sight, It fills me with fright And try as I might – I HATE MEAT!
	(sternly)	But if anyone asks, My name is Bernard And I'm fearsomely, awesomely scary!

MUSICAL SCORE – page 69

THE SOUTH OF FRANCE

DIRECTOR'S NOTES

 TOPIC. The Camargue, complete with wild white horses and little black bulls, flamingoes and salt lakes.

 TOPIC. Provence and the perfume industry with its lavender-growing centre at Grasse.

 TOPIC. The Alpes-Maritimes and the olive groves. The islands (including Corsica – and we know who was born there, don't we? See **LET'S GO OVER**). The Monte Carlo rally – and there's plenty more to discover.

THE SONG

 SING IT. In the south of France,
It's so warm and dry,
Not a cloud to be seen in a dusty sky.
I'm so hot, says the sea, with a gusty sigh.

MUSICAL SCORE – page 72

I'M A TREE

DIRECTOR'S NOTES

So here's the last number in this episode before the **SING IT AND SAY IT** finale.

 SING IT. This is a speedy song requiring tongue-twisting expertise with the 'echo' lines in brackets. The little cherubs in the backing group (The Trunkettes? The Palmettes? The St Tropez Singers? No Cannes Do?) will need to concentrate – but the effect is very entertaining if they can't quite manage the words. It is certainly quick, so don't worry!

 TOPIC. We've included history content (Romans, Hannibal), geographical references (Monaco, St Tropez) and a touch of Hollywood (Marilyn Monroe, Brigitte Bardot).

 ART & CRAFT. Plenty of opportunities for art and craft input here – palm tree costumes, sandy seafront backdrop, sunshine, Romans, elephants, handfuls of 1000-franc notes for the multi-millionaires. Yes, it would be lovely to fly to Cannes and make a video on the beach instead, but I'd say your chances were non-exis – er, slim.

DRAMA. Characterisation galore is available for staging this song. Jean-Louis, the backing palms, film stars, directors tanned and grand, Romans, Hannibal, elephants, millionaires – enough roles for the entire class – or entire school.

Have fun with Jean-Louis – we have!

THE SONG

 SING IT.   You can call me Jean-Louis,
Jean-Louis, Jean-Louis, Jean-Louis, Jean-Louis.
I have brains and bonhomie,
Bonhomie, bonhomie, bonhomie, bonhomie
And as you can probably see,
You can see, you can see, you can see, you can see,
I'm a tree, but what a tree,
What a tree, what a tree, what a tree, what a tree.

I have wit and I have charm,
He has charm, he has charm, he has charm, he has charm.
Superchic and supercalm,
Supercalm, supercalm, supercalm, supercalm.
I'm so pleased to meet you Ma'am,
Meet you Ma'am, meet you Ma'am,
        meet you Ma'am, meet you Ma'am.
I'm a palm, but what a palm,
What a palm, what a palm, what a palm, what a palm.

Once the south of France was home
To the citizens of Rome
And the elephants came by
What a smell, what a smell, what a smell, what a smell!
Under Hannibal's war cry.
Monaco's around the bay,
Multi-millionaires at play,
Either there or St Tropez,
Spending money night and day.

I'm involved in cinema,
Cinema, cinema, cinema, cinema.
I'm the greatest palm tree star,
Palm tree star, palm tree star, palm tree star, palm tree star
For directors, tanned and grand,
Tanned and grand, tanned and grand,
        tanned and grand, tanned and grand,
Making movies on the sand
On the sand, on the sand, on the sand, on the sand.

I've met Marilyn Monroe
Marilyn, Marilyn, Marilyn, Marilyn
And the great Brigitte Bardot
Ooh là là! Ooh là là! Ooh là là! Ooh là là!
They were proud to star with me,
Star with him, star with him, star with him? STAR WITH HIM?
I'm a tree, but what a tree!
What a tree, what a tree, what a tree, what a tree!

MUSICAL SCORE – page 73

SING IT AND SAY IT (Finale)

 SING IT. We're good to you, aren't we? Not a lot of extra work involved here, we promise. You and your class already know the words for the closing number because it was also the opening number. Now, come along, it was only ten minutes ago!

 SING IT. An option to replace One, Two, Three – Four! with Un, Deux, Trois – Quatre! if you feel like a final French flavour.

 DRAMA. The repeat of the last line creates a rousing finish. We suggest a pantomime-style deep bow or similar theatrical flourish at this point before the audience storms the stage for autographs!

 TOPIC. Organise your class to write 30 words each, giving their impressions of this **SING IT AND SAY IT** episode. It's a very useful exercise and we always find the results fascinating. If you'd like to pass on their insights and comments to us, we'd be delighted to hear from you – and your class.

THE SONG

 SING IT. Sing it and say it, can anyone play it?
There's no need to be shy.
Sing it and say it, can anyone play it?
Come on, let's give it a try.

You'll soon learn the tune in a jiff and a half,
You'll soon learn the words, they might make you laugh!

So listen to me, there's no need to read,
Rhyme and rhythm are all you need –

 SAY IT. Sing it with me on the count of three –
One, two, three, four!

 SING IT. Sing it and say it, can anyone play it?
There's no need to be shy.
Sing it and say it, can anyone play it?
Come on, let's give it a,
Let's give it a,
Let's give it a try!

MUSICAL SCORE – page 79

FRANCE'S FOUR CORNERS

SING IT AND SAY IT

Easily

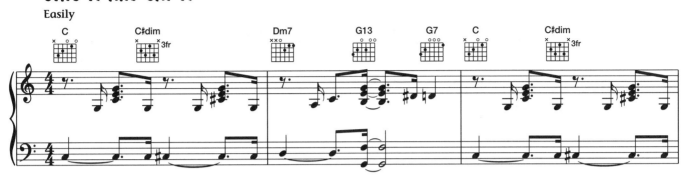

Sing it and say it, can a-ny-one play it?__ There's no need to be

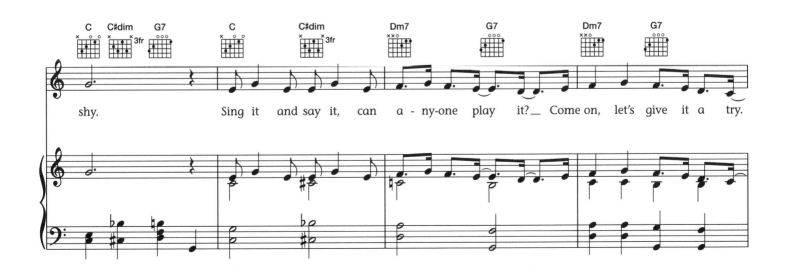

shy.   Sing it and say it, can a-ny-one play it?__ Come on, let's give it a try.

THE WEST OF FRANCE

Western France tempo

LASCAUX

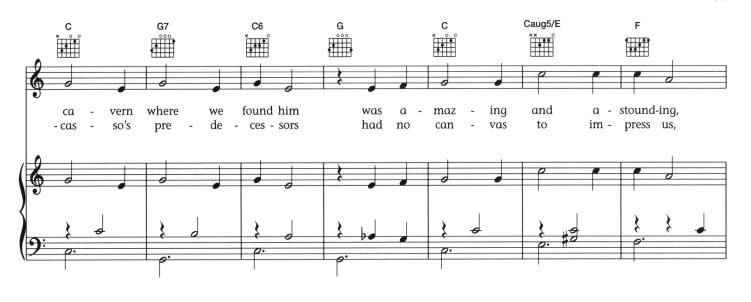

ca - vern where we found him was a - maz - ing and a - stound-ing,
-cas - so's pre - de - ces - sors had no can - vas to im - press us,

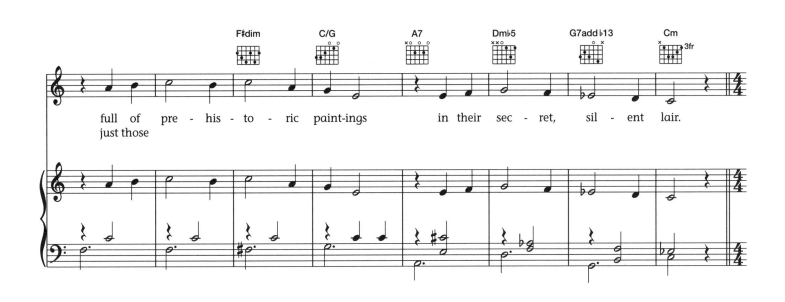

full of pre - his - to - ric paint-ings in their sec - ret, sil - ent lair.
just those

Monster tempo (Slow, getting faster)

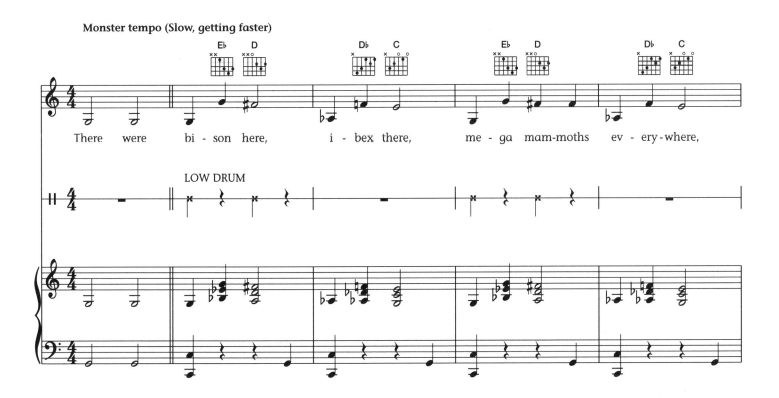

There were bi - son here, i - bex there, me - ga mam-moths ev - ery-where,

LOW DRUM

THE NORTH OF FRANCE

Northern France tempo

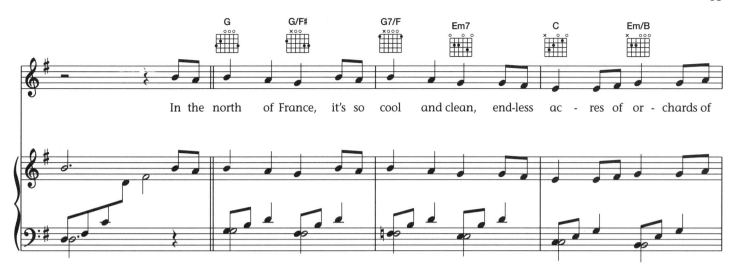

In the north of France, it's so cool and clean, end-less ac - res of or - chards of

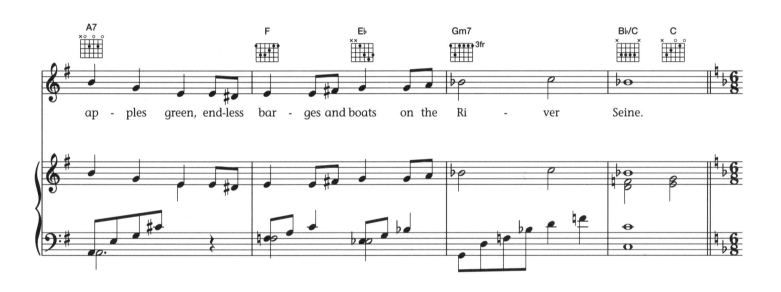

ap - ples green, end-less bar - ges and boats on the Ri - ver Seine.

BARGES ON THE SEINE

River/Canal tempo

BRIGITTE

Bon - jour, bon-jour to you!

CHIME BARS

BARGE CHORUS

Liv - ing on the Ri - ver Seine, hard at work all day. Wait un - til the

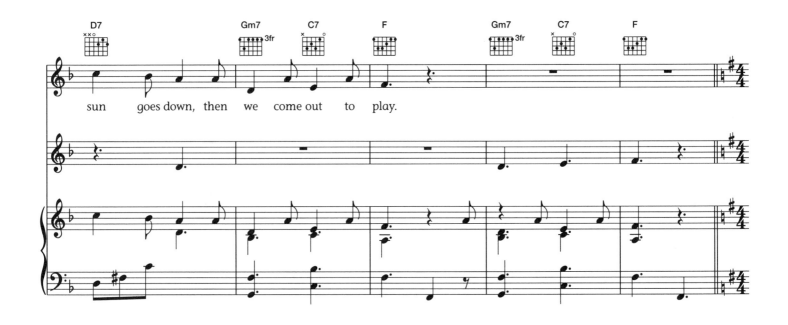

sun goes down, then we come out to play.

THE EAST OF FRANCE

East of France tempo

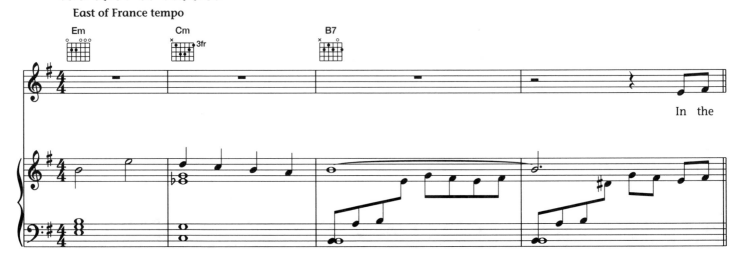

In the

east of France where the moun - tains rise, there is snow on Mont Blanc, e - ven in Ju - ly and the

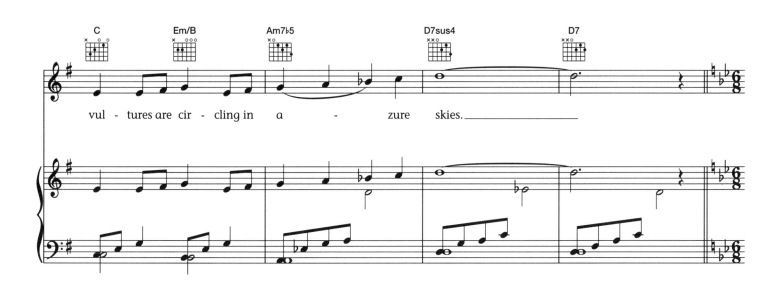

vul - tures are cir - cling in a - zure skies._____

BERNARD

Vegetarian tempo

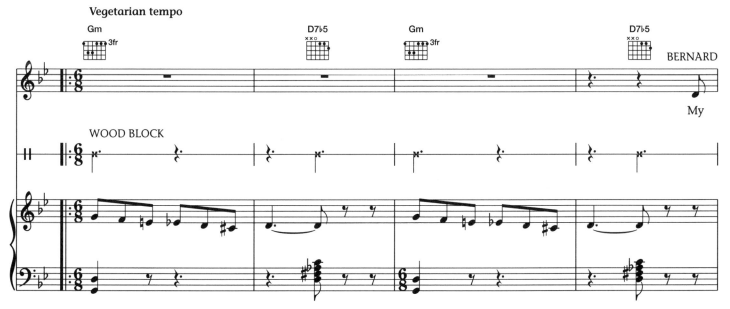

BERNARD

My

WOOD BLOCK

name is Ber-nard.   I'm   fear-some - ly,   awe-some - ly   sca - ry.   To
As   a   vul - ture, I'm   real - ly   not   va - lid.   I

tell   you   the   truth,   of   these   moun-tains, I'm   ter - ri - bly   wa - ry.   I
ought to   pick bones,   but   I'd   ra - ther have quiche and   a   sa - lad.   I

have   to   be   sca - ry,   you   see,   it's   sim - ply   ex - pect - ed   of   me.   It's   a
have   to   eat   car - rion,   you   see,   it's   sim - ply   ex - pect - ed   of   me.

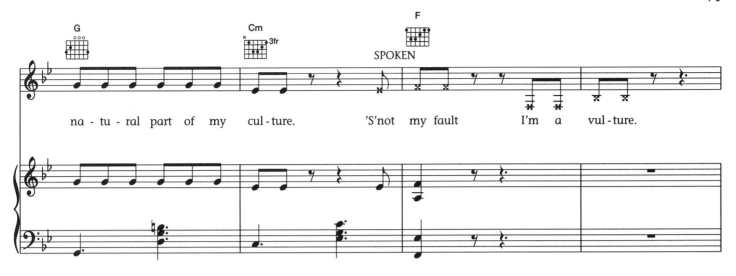

na-tu-ral part of my cul-ture. 'S'not my fault I'm a vul-ture.

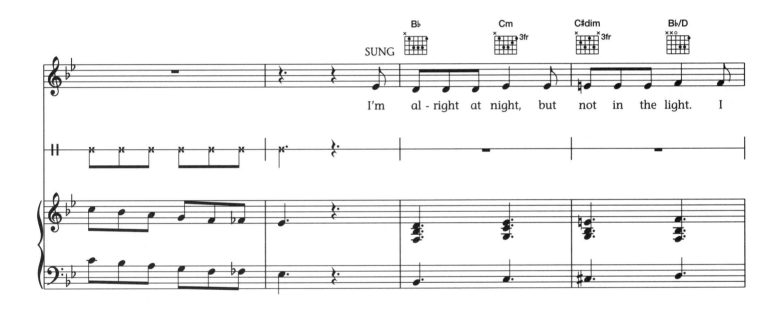

I'm al-right at night, but not in the light. I

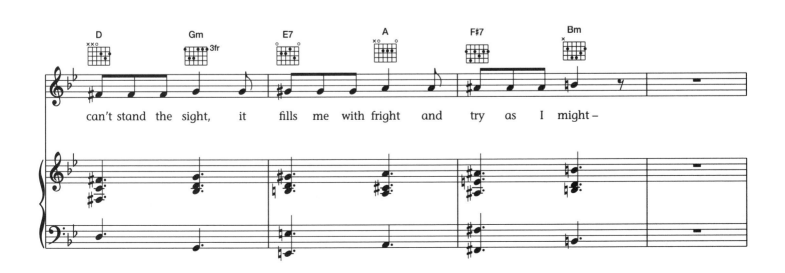

can't stand the sight, it fills me with fright and try as I might—

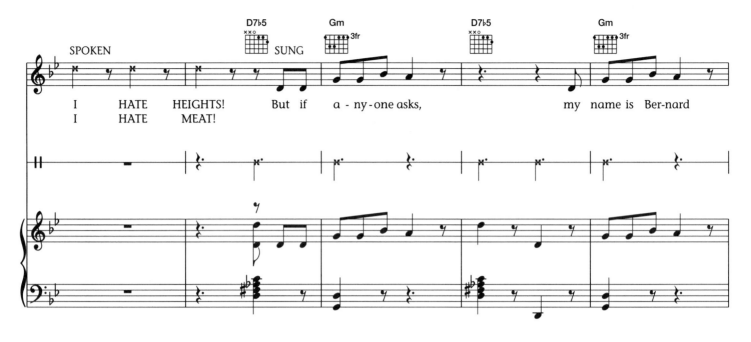

I HATE HEIGHTS! But if a-ny-one asks, my name is Ber-nard
I HATE MEAT!

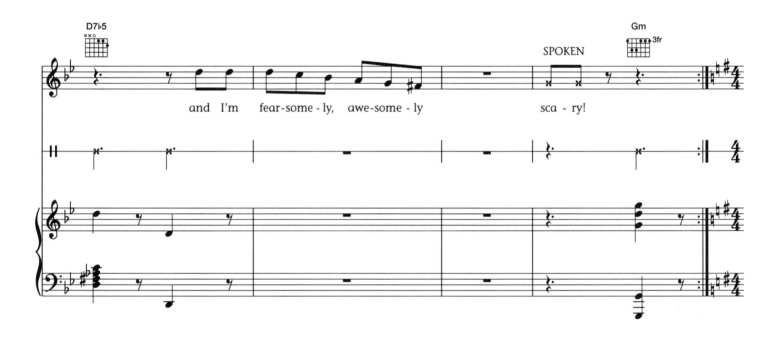

and I'm fear-some-ly, awe-some-ly sca-ry!

THE SOUTH OF FRANCE

Balmy

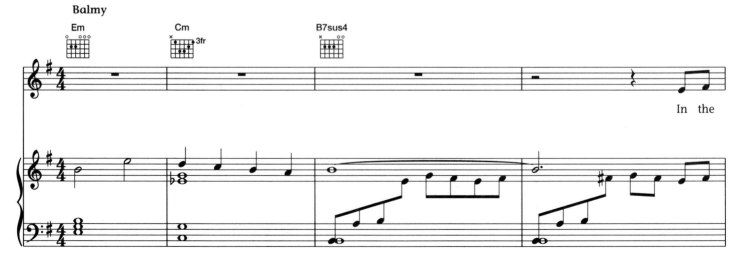

In the

south of France, it's so warm and dry, not a cloud to be seen in a dust - y sky. I'm so

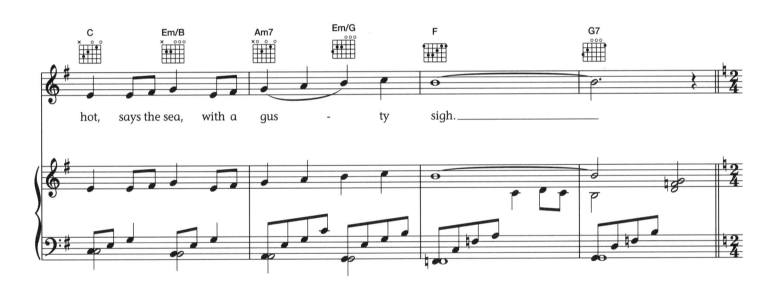

hot, says the sea, with a gus - ty sigh._____

I'M A TREE

A la hip palm tree

JEAN-LOUIS

You can call me Jean - Lou -

Once the south of France was home_____ to the ci - ti -
bay,_____ mul - ti - mil - lion -

palm.

- zens of Rome_____ and the e - le -
- aires at play,_____ ei - ther there or

- phants came by_____ un - der Han - ni -
St Tro - pez,_____ spend-ing mo - ney

what a smell, what a smell, what a smell, what a smell!

-bal's war cry. _____ Mo - na - co's a - round the

night and day. _____ I'm in - volved in ci - ne -

-ma,
-roe

I'm the great - est
and the great Bri -

ci - ne - ma, ci - ne - ma, ci - ne - ma, ci - ne - ma.
Ma - ri - lyn, Ma - ri - lyn, Ma - ri - lyn, Ma - ri - lyn

sand, _____ I've met Mar - il - yn Mon -

on the sand, on the sand, on the sand, on the sand.

what a tree! _____

what a tree, what a tree, what a tree, what a tree!

SING IT AND SAY IT

Easily

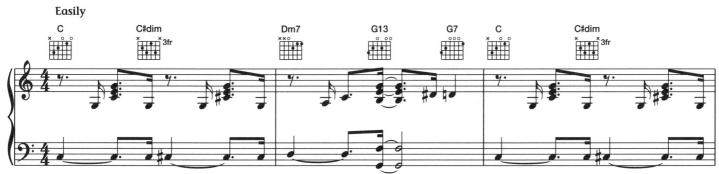

3   LET'S GO OVER

CONTENTS

In this episode, we join a class of English children and their teacher on a trip to France to meet their pen-friends. They 'cha-cha' over the Channel in style with **LET'S GO OVER!**

In **ACHETER!**, we take a whirlwind tour of the food stores followed by a 'round' about everyone's age (teacher excluded), then a look at the weather and seasons, including the colours of the rainbow, in both French and English.

Next, a helping of l'histoire. Allow us to introduce you to a regiment of **BONAPARTE'S BOYS**, Napoleon's trusty troops and then to present the talents of **THE IMPRESSIONISTS**, both painters and composers.

We finish on a giggle with the intriguingly titled **FRIED APPLE**.

A rousing finale of **SING IT AND SAY IT** ends our visit.

SING IT AND SAY IT

DIRECTOR'S NOTES

Our first song expresses the essence of the **SING IT AND SAY IT** project:

SING IT.   Singing easy-to-learn music
SAY IT.   Saying entertaining words with rhyme and rhythm
PLAY IT.   Playing simple accompaniments

We'd add **BUILDING** to that list. Building confidence, vocabulary and musical ability. Building concentration and timing, teamwork and, that elusive quality, discipline!

The other term which encapsulates **SING IT AND SAY IT** is FUN. Fun in learning *and* fun in teaching

 SING IT.   The first and last sections of this song are identical for easy learning and, (with a small change to the last section), the whole song is repeated at the end of this 10-minute episode.

 SING IT.   **SING IT AND SAY IT** can be performed as an ensemble, in separate groups or as a solo.

 FX.   Clapping and clicking of fingers will find their natural places in this song.

 DRAMA.   However you use the material, your class will have plenty of suggestions for actions and simple dance routines. Someone will want to be the conductor and everyone will want to shout 'Four!' (after One, Two, Three). Let them, they're learning!

THE SONG

 SING IT.   Sing it and say it, can anyone play it?
There's no need to be shy.
Sing it and say it, can anyone play it?
Come on, let's give it a try.

You'll soon learn the tune in a jiff and a half,
You'll soon learn the words, they might make you laugh!

So listen to me, there's no need to read,
Rhyme and rhythm are all you need –

 SAY IT.   Sing it with me on the count of three –
One, two, three, four!

 SING IT.   Sing it and say it, can anyone play it?
There's no need to be shy.
Sing it and say it, can anyone play it?
Come on, let's give it a try.

MUSICAL SCORE – page 98

LET'S GO OVER

DIRECTOR'S NOTES

A cheerful little number to put you in the holiday mood.

 SING IT. Divide your class into groups for this if you like. We don't mind at all.

 TOPIC. Vast opportunities for wallcharts, maps and route planners here, of course. Why not organise the class to write to one of the ferry companies for info packs? Or off to the local travel agents for another raid.

 TOPIC. Project time. Who's been on a ferry? Who's going on one? Encourage them to save tickets, brochures and boarding passes for their scrapbooks. Ask them to take photos or draw what they saw.

 ART & CRAFT. You love this bit, don't you? Crossing to France could be achieved in a cardboard ferry or cut-out boat.

 ART & CRAFT. Make Union Jacks and Tricolour flags with the class. How about a cleverly-constructed Big Ben and Eiffel Tower? Waves painted on placards? Wafts of green and blue material to represent the sea? Or should it be grey and brown material to represent the sea?

 ART & CRAFT. Make some shakers from dried beans in a plastic bottle, milk-bottle tops in a carton, paper clips in a tin.

 PLAY IT. Go percussive with those shakers! See Musical Score (page 100).

THE SONG

 SAY IT.

MADAME:	Bonjour, la classe!
CLASS:	Bonjour, Madame!
MADAME:	Let's go over
CLASS:	to France!

 SING IT.   Let's go over from Dover
To Calais in no time at all.
Hop on a ferry at Folkestone,
Disembark at Boulogne's harbour wall.

From Weymouth or Worthing or Portsmouth
To Cherbourg or even Dieppe,
Or Le Havre where the River Seine meets with the sea,
The journey is just the first step.

Ooh là là!

MUSICAL SCORE – page 100

ACHETER!

DIRECTOR'S NOTES

 SAY IT.   Acheter! Definitely sounds like a sneeze to us!

 DRAMA.   So it's off to the shops for provisions. We envisage the smallest person in the group being loaded up with boxes of pastries, bags of vegetables and armfuls of baguettes until he/she can't see out. This miniature pack-pony staggers off at the end of the number to an off-stage crash. Oh dear, must be our warped sense of the silly.

 TOPIC.   Other shops could be given the same singing treatment: Pharmacie, Poissonerie, Boucherie etc. We'll leave your class to think of the others.

 ART & CRAFT.   Papier mâché veg, cardboard shopfronts, moustaches for shopkeepers etc.

 PLAY IT.   Coins jingling in a pocket – or a sock – are fun with this shopping song. Just as long as the sock full of francs doesn't develop cosh-like tendencies in small hands . . .

(cont.)

THE SONG

 SAY IT.

MADAME:	Now that we're over in France,
	Let's say hello to our friends.
ENGLISH CLASS:	How do you do?
FRENCH CLASS:	Comment ça va?
ENGLISH CLASS:	How do you do?
FRENCH CLASS:	Comment ça va?

 SING IT.

FRENCH CHILD:	Acheter!
ENGLISH CHILD:	Bless you!
FRENCH CHILD:	Acheter!
ENGLISH CHILD:	Bless you!
FRENCH CHILD:	Acheter!
ENGLISH CHILD:	What did you say?
FRENCH CHILD:	Let's go shopping today!
ENSEMBLE:	Acheter! Acheter! Let's go shopping today!
ENGLISH CHILD:	Where to?
FRENCH CHILD:	Pâtisserie!
ENGLISH CHILD:	Pardon me?
FRENCH CHILD:	Pâtisserie!
ENGLISH CHILD:	Pardon me?
FRENCH CHILD:	Pâtisserie!
ENGLISH CHILD:	What can it be?
ENGLISH CHILD 2:	A pastry shop for me!
ENSEMBLE:	Acheter! Acheter! Let's go shopping today!
ENGLISH CHILD:	Where to now?
FRENCH CHILD:	L'épicerie!
ENGLISH CHILD:	Say it again.
FRENCH CHILD:	L'épicerie!
ENGLISH CHILD:	Say it again.
FRENCH CHILD:	L'épicerie!
ENGLISH CHILD:	What can it be?
ENGLISH CHILD 2:	A grocery shop – come and see!
ENSEMBLE:	Acheter! Acheter! Let's go shopping today!
ENGLISH CHILD:	Where to now?
FRENCH CHILD:	Boulangerie!
ENGLISH CHILD:	Don't ask me.
FRENCH CHILD:	Boulangerie!
ENGLISH CHILD:	Don't ask me.
FRENCH CHILD:	Boulangerie!
ENGLISH CHILD:	What can it be?
ENGLISH CHILD 2:	A shop full of bread for our tea!
ENSEMBLE:	Acheter! Acheter! We've been shopping today!
	Acheter! Acheter! We've been shopping today!

MUSICAL SCORE – <u>page 102</u>

QUEL AGE AS TU?

DIRECTOR'S NOTES

The musical credit for this song belongs to Cheron Mole. Thanks, Cher!

 SING IT. This round can be sung in all French, all English, French first or English first.

 DRAMA. The music alone suggests simply swaying dance movements.

 DRAMA. Substitute the ages of your class to suit.

 DRAMA. Try staging this with different groups of children moving forward to sing then stepping aside to allow the next group through.

 PLAY IT. As far as the piano score is concerned, there are basically two chords to conquer and that's it!

 PLAY IT. This is pretty with chime bars. See Musical Score (page 106).

THE SONG

 SING IT.

Quel âge as tu?
Quel âge as tu?
How old are you?
How old are you?

J'ai cinq ans.
J'ai cinq ans.
I am five.
I am five.

Mon ami a sept ans.
Mon ami a sept ans.
My friend is seven.
My friend is seven.

Presque huit.
Presque huit.
Nearly eight.
Nearly eight.

MUSICAL SCORE – page 106

SEASONS

DIRECTOR'S NOTES

 TOPIC. Encourage your class to watch the weather on television and spot the meteorological symbols over France.

 TOPIC. Ask them to find snow reports from the ski resorts for France in the newspapers and bring them in to school (not a good project for July).

 TOPIC. Look at minimum and maximum temperatures, sun/rain hours, wind speeds and unusual weather. Has there ever been a hurricane or tornado in France? Blizzards, storms and bizarre items like small green frogs in rainfall, frost fairs and avalanches all make for interesting projects.

 ART & CRAFT. Placards or hand-painted T-shirts for the different weather symbols. Thought you'd appreciate that bit.

 SING IT. Sing this in 2 groups, 8 groups or use 4 soloists for each language.

 PLAY IT. Break out the chime bars for this song. See Musical Score (page 108).

THE SONG

 SAY IT. MADAME: Attention, la classe! Les Saisons!

 SING IT.

FRENCH GROUP:	Il fait chaud,
ENGLISH GROUP:	Il fait chaud.
FRENCH GROUP:	C'est l'été,
ENGLISH GROUP:	C'est l'été.
	In summer, it's hot.
FRENCH GROUP:	We have the same weather as you.
FRENCH GROUP:	Il fait du vent,
ENGLISH GROUP:	Il fait du vent.
FRENCH GROUP:	C'est l'automne,
ENGLISH GROUP:	C'est l'automne.
	In autumn, it blows.
FRENCH GROUP:	We have the same weather as you.
FRENCH GROUP:	Il neige,
ENGLISH GROUP:	Il neige.
FRENCH GROUP:	C'est l'hiver,
ENGLISH GROUP:	C'est l'hiver.
	In winter, it snows.
FRENCH GROUP:	We have the same weather as you.
FRENCH GROUP:	Il pleut,
ENGLISH GROUP:	Il pleut.
FRENCH GROUP:	C'est le printemps,
ENGLISH GROUP:	C'est le printemps.
	In springtime, it's wet.
FRENCH GROUP:	We have the same weather as you.
BOTH GROUPS:	We have the same weather as you!

MUSICAL SCORE – page 108

RAINBOW

 DRAMA. Dress 7 children in the colours of the rainbow and heaven knows what might happen. The ball's in your court.

 TOPIC. We tried to think of a memory-prompting rhyme for the colours of the rainbow in French (like Richard Of York Gave Blood In Vain – or is it Vein?) but then we decided it would be a better idea to leave it to your pupils' imaginations.

 SING IT. Violet is pronounced vee-o-lay, in case you were wondering. And if you weren't, it's still pronounced vee-o-lay!

 PLAY IT. Percussion-wise, it's triangle time. At least you don't have to MAKE a triangle. See Musical Score (page 111).

THE SONG

 SING IT.

FRENCH GROUP:	Qu'est-ce que c'est que ça?
ENGLISH GROUP:	Whatever can that be? We call it a rainbow.
FRENCH GROUP:	Un arc-en-ciel, mais oui!
ENGLISH GROUP:	An arch in the sky?
FRENCH GROUP:	Un arc-en-ciel. An arch in the sky, mais oui!
FRENCH GROUP:	Quelles couleurs vois-tu?
ENGLISH GROUP:	What colours can you see? All the shades of the rainbow.
FRENCH GROUP:	Un arc-en-ciel, mais oui!
ENGLISH GROUP:	Red!
FRENCH GROUP:	Rouge!
ENGLISH GROUP:	Orange!
FRENCH GROUP:	Orange!
ENGLISH GROUP:	Yellow!
FRENCH GROUP:	Jaune!
ENGLISH GROUP:	Green!
FRENCH GROUP:	Vert!
ENGLISH GROUP:	Blue!
FRENCH GROUP:	Bleu!
ENGLISH GROUP:	Indigo!
FRENCH GROUP:	Indigo!
ENGLISH GROUP:	Violet!
FRENCH GROUP:	Violet!

MUSICAL SCORE – page 111

BONAPARTE'S BOYS

DIRECTOR'S NOTES

 DRAMA.   Unlimited troops can take part in this military extravaganza.

 SING IT.   A good strong marching song.

 DRAMA.   Uniforms? Depends if you feel like incurring the concentrated wrath of every soldier's Mum!

 TOPIC.   Yes, Napoleon reputedly did plant poplar trees along the roads of France to march his troops in the shade. You think we make this stuff up, don't you? It's true, honestly. Well, we can't have the lads sunbathing on the way to invade Prussia, can we? They weren't there to enjoy themselves, after all.

 DRAMA.   Plenty of clap, stamp and march.

 DRAMA.   Choose the megalomaniac in your class to play Napoleon at the head of his army. Now, are you grateful we didn't mention his horse as a character?

 TOPIC.   Plenty of material here. Wellington and Waterloo, Nelson and Trafalgar, the Battle of the Nile, Josephine, Corsica, exile to Elba and St Helena.

 PLAY IT.   Beat that side-drum! Ear plugs at the ready. See Musical Score (page 114).

 DRAMA.   A little drummer boy (or girl) marching ahead of the corps is fun, preferably one with a reasonable sense of rhythm or you'll have Bonaparte's Boys bearing black eyes and bruises.

THE SONG

 SAY IT. MADAME: Attention, la classe! L'histoire!

 SING IT. We're the boys in Napoleon's army, marching two abreast.
We're fearless Frenchmen, our medals on our chest.
In battle, we're unbeatable!
In battle, we're the best!

Because we're Bonaparte's Boys, Bonaparte's Braves,
Napoleon's men for the rest of our days!
Bonaparte's Boys, Bonaparte's Braves,
Our enemies call us Napoleon's Knaves!

 SAY IT.
ENGLISH CHILD:	When was he born?
SOLDIERS:	1769!
ENGLISH CHILD:	Where was he born?
SOLDIERS:	Corsica!

 SING IT. We're the boys in Napoleon's army, we've really got it made.
These poplar trees he planted to keep us in the shade
And as we march to victory, we know that we'll be paid.

Because we're Bonaparte's Boys, Bonaparte's Braves,
Napoleon's men for the rest of our days!
Bonaparte's Boys, Bonaparte's Braves,
Our enemies call us Napoleon's Knaves!

MUSICAL SCORE – page 114

THE IMPRESSIONISTS

DIRECTOR'S NOTES

Firstly, we must pay homage to Erik Satie, from whose work, 'Gymnopedie', inspiration was drawn for this song.

 TOPIC. It would definitely be worth acquiring a copy of Satie's work and asking your class for their impressions (pun intended).

 TOPIC. Take them on a tour of the Impressionist painters if you can. Use postcards, calendars or posters unless your school can run to a gallery visit. Ask the class to visit their local library and look in the Adults' art section for info on Monet, Manet, Cézanne, Gauguin etc. Buy or borrow an Art magazine for more material.

 ART & CRAFT. Have a go at explaining the style, the use of light and the 'spots and dots, splash and dash' approach. Best (and messiest) of all, get them to try copying a masterpiece or making up their own. Then close the door on them and go for a coffee, before coming back to clear up the chaos. Sorry, that was an irresponsible piece of advice. Ignore us, we're suffering from yellow ochre-speckled spectacle lenses!

 PLAY IT. Play Debussy's Clair de Lune for the class – on the piano if you can manage it. If not, borrow the CD from the library.

 DRAMA. We envisage the staging of this song with two different age groups of children. Or separate groups of boys and girls. The girls (or older group) are trying to tell us, in a mature and slightly serious fashion, all about the Impressionists. Then the boys (or younger group) bounce on stage in unsophisticated style with 'spots and dots', to the irritation of the first group. Peace is restored for the second verse, then disrupted again for the chorus. A 'Big Sister, Annoying Little Brother' scenario.

 SAY IT. Interesting names and phrases here plus mouthfuls of spots and dots to twist young tongues around.

 FX. Clapping during chorus.

THE SONG

 SING IT.

Pierre Renoir and Claude Monet,
Famous painters of their day,
Working in a new creative way.
In old straw hats and cotton smocks,
Painting lily ponds and locks,
Poppy fields and dandelion clocks.

With lots and lots of spots and dots,
They formed Impressions made from lots
And lots and lots and lots and lots of spots and lots of dots!
Occasionally a splash, occasionally a dash,
But mostly lots and lots and lots of spots and dots!

Ravel, Satie and Debussy,
Great composers of their day,
Writing in a new creative way.
In Satie's three Gymnopedies
And Claire de Lune by Debussy,
They painted sound that we can hear and see.

With lots and lots of spots and dots,
They formed Impressions made from lots
And lots and lots and lots and lots of spots and lots of dots!
Occasionally a splash, occasionally a crash,
But mostly lots and lots and lots of spots and dots!

MUSICAL SCORE – page 117

FRIED APPLE

DIRECTOR'S NOTES

 SING IT. Short, but sweet, this piece is designed to make a couple of French words stick in the memory by sheer silliness – sorry, taste association.

 DRAMA. The characters could be sitting on a step or a five-bar gate, in l'épicerie looking at the fruit and veg or sharing a pique-nique.

 DRAMA. The girl is resignedly patient and the boy is perfectly puzzled, but realisation is dawning on him. Slowly. Naturally, the roles are interchangeable.

 DRAMA. The girl has a natural Gallic shrug and by the time the boy reaches 'Zut!' (see glossary), he has adopted her habit.

Thanks to Caroline Coxon for reminding us of 'Zut!'

THE SONG

 SING IT. ENGLISH BOY: If une pomme is an apple
And la terre is the ground –

FRENCH GIRL: Oui!

ENGLISH BOY: Pomme de terre is potato
And pomme de terre sounds
Like an apple
That someone's dug up
From the ground –

FRENCH GIRL: Oui, c'est ça!
Pomme de terre!
Potato to you!

 SAY IT. ENGLISH BOY: Does this mean my chips will taste of apple?
Zut!

MUSICAL SCORE – page 119

SING IT AND SAY IT (Finale)

DIRECTOR'S NOTES

 SING IT. We're good to you, aren't we? Not a lot of extra work involved here, we promise. You and your class already know the words for the closing number because it was also the opening number. Now, come along, it was only ten minutes ago!

 SING IT. An option to replace One, Two, Three – Four! with Un, Deux, Trois – Quatre! if you feel like a final French flavour.

 DRAMA. The repeat of the last line creates a rousing finish. We suggest a pantomime-style deep bow or similar theatrical flourish at this point before the audience storms the stage for autographs!

 TOPIC. Organise your class to write 30 words each, giving their impressions of this **SING IT AND SAY IT** episode. It's a very useful exercise and we always find the results fascinating. If you'd like to pass on their insights and comments to us, we'd be delighted to hear from you – and your class.

We seriously hope that you, your pupils and your audience thoroughly enjoyed the **SING IT AND SAY IT** experience and that you'll be working with us again soon. We look forward to it. Sing on!

THE SONG

 SING IT. Sing it and say it, can anyone play it?
There's no need to be shy.
Sing it and say it, can anyone play it?
Come on, let's give it a try.

You'll soon learn the tune in a jiff and a half,
You'll soon learn the words, they might make you laugh!

So listen to me, there's no need to read,
Rhyme and rhythm are all you need –

 SAY IT. Sing it with me on the count of three –
One, two, three, four!

 SING IT. Sing it and say it, can anyone play it?
There's no need to be shy.
Sing it and say it, can anyone play it?
Come on, let's give it a,
Let's give it a,
Let's give it a try!

MUSICAL SCORE – page 120

LET'S GO OVER

SING IT AND SAY IT

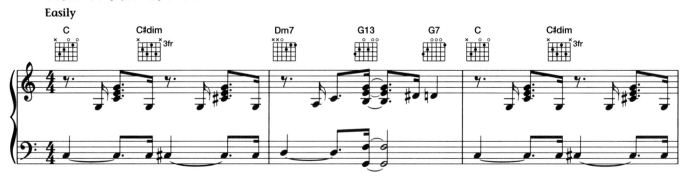

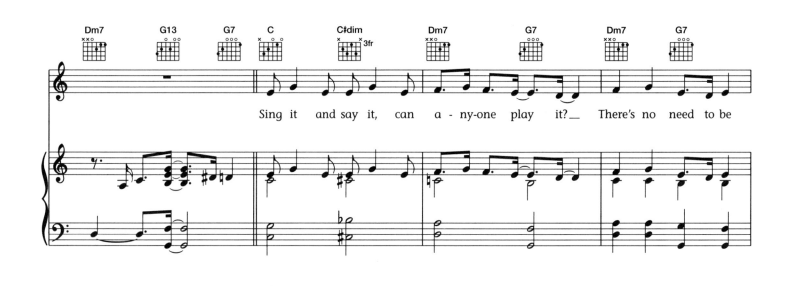

Sing it and say it, can a-ny-one play it?__ There's no need to be

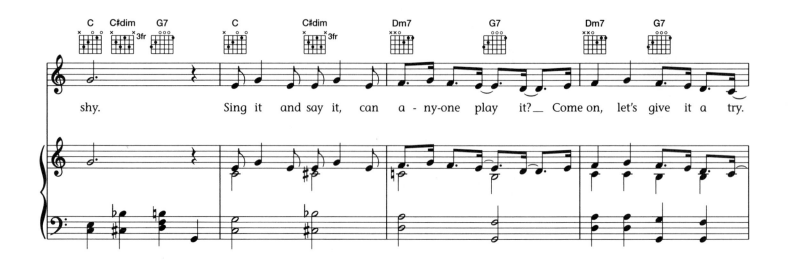

shy. Sing it and say it, can a-ny-one play it?__ Come on, let's give it a try.

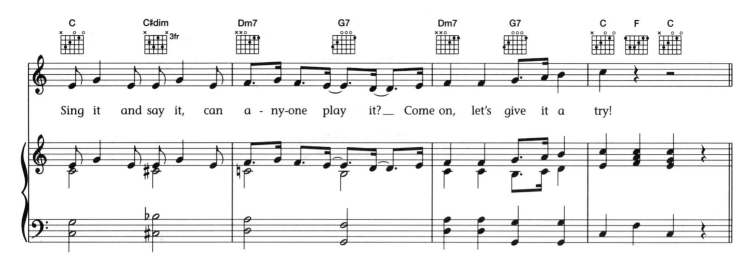

LET'S GO OVER

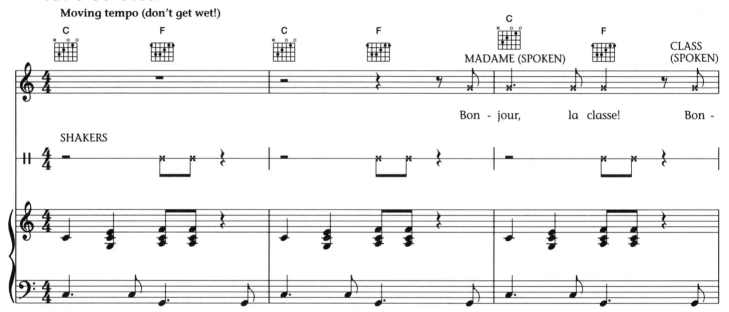

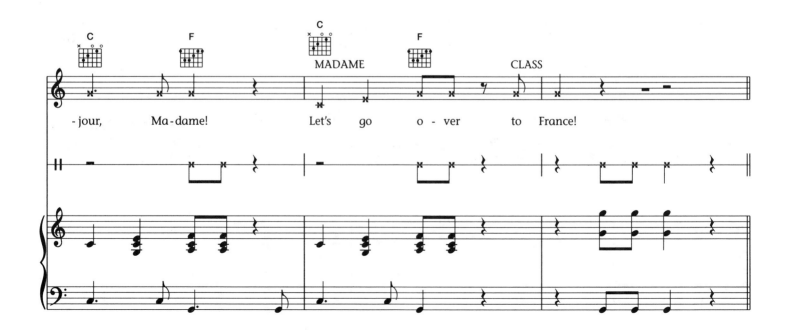

101

QUEL AGE AS TU?

SEASONS

have the same wea-ther as you. Il pleut, il pleut. C'est le

prin - temps, c'est le prin - temps. In spring - time, __ it's wet. We

have the same wea-ther as you. We have the same wea-ther as you!

RAINBOW

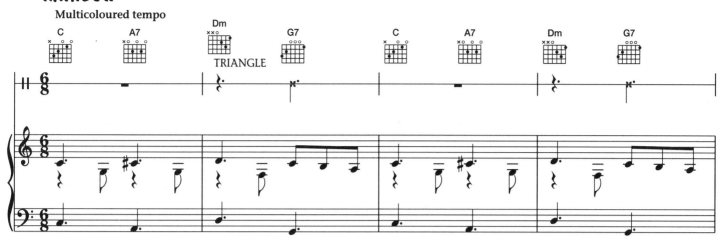
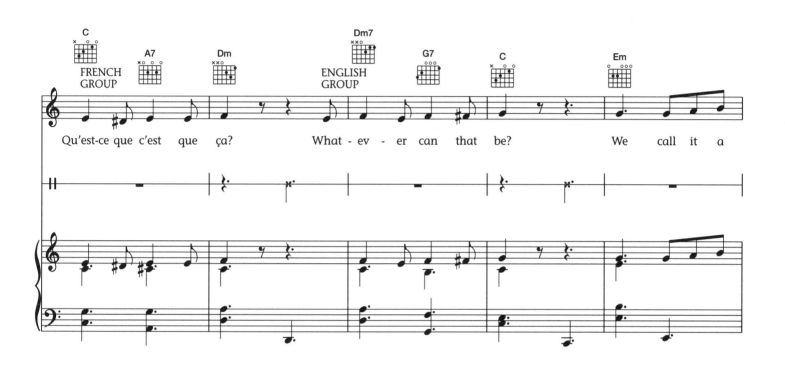
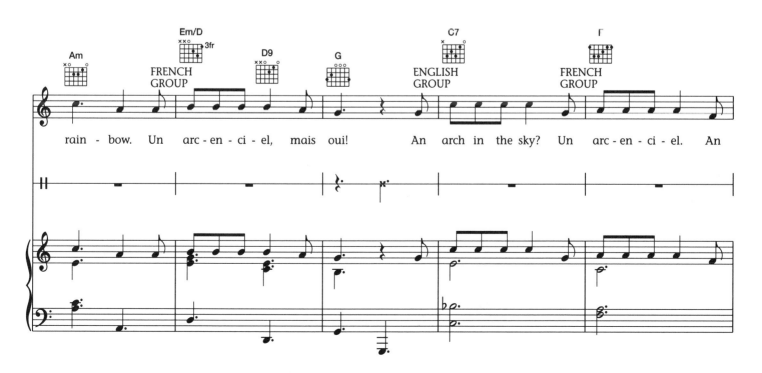

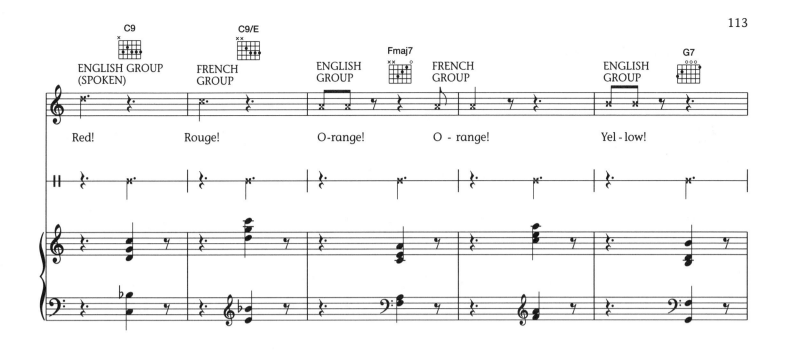

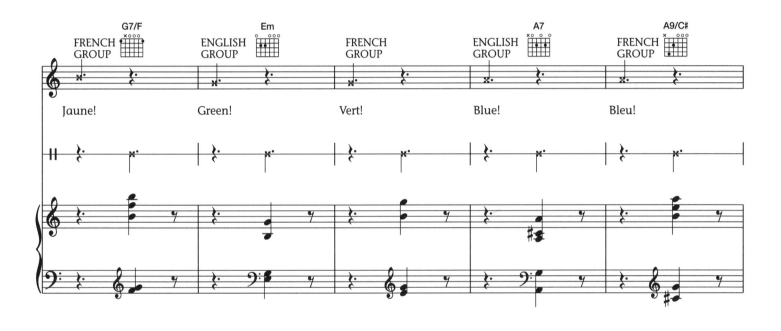

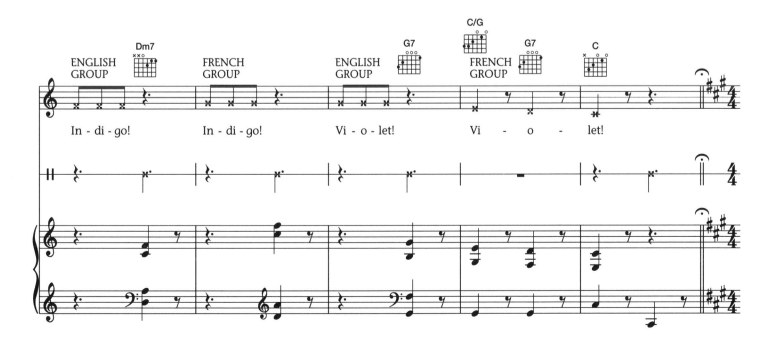

BONAPARTE'S BOYS

THE IMPRESSIONISTS

A la Satie

-ca-sion-ally a dash, but most-ly lots and lots and lots of spots and dots!
crash,

FRIED APPLE

Questioning tempo

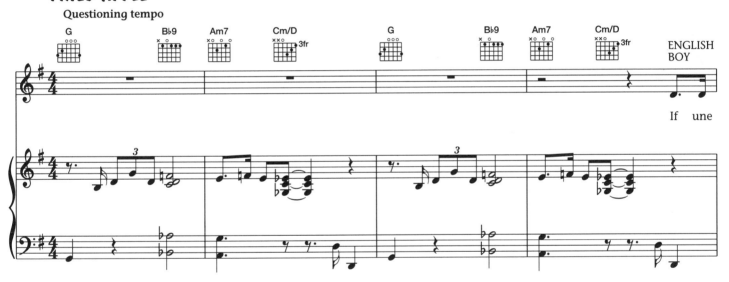

ENGLISH BOY

If une

pomme is an ap - ple and la terre is the ground— Oui!

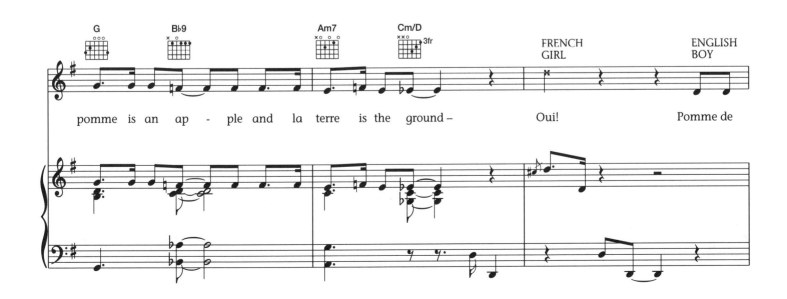

FRENCH GIRL

ENGLISH BOY

Pomme de

terre is po-ta-to____ and pomme de terre sounds like an ap-ple that some-one's_ dug

up from the ground – Oui, c'est ça! Pomme de terre! Po-ta-to____ to____ you!

FRENCH GIRL
(SPOKEN)

ENGLISH
BOY

Does this mean my chips will taste of ap-ple? Zut!

SING IT AND SAY IT

Easily

GLOSSARY

1 LET'S MEET MAURICE

FRENCH	ENGLISH	PRONUNCIATION
Bonjour	Good day, Hello	Bonn-jore
Mon père	My Dad	Monn pear (Like the fruit)
La mère	Mum	La mare (No, Mum doesn't have the face of a horse)
La mer	The sea	La mare (More horses! Seahorses?)
Bienvenu	Welcome	Beyan-ver-noo
Je m'appelle	I am called My name is	Je ma-pell
Ma belle France	My beautiful France	Ma bell Frahns
Venez à Paris	Come to Paris	Ve-nay a Paree
Et maintenant	And now	Ay-manta-non
Voici les mains	Here are some hands	Vwa-see lay mehn (No connection to mains drainage/electricity)
Tu ne me comprends pas	You don't understand me	Too nuh muh comm-pron pah
Ce sont des mains	These are hands	Suh sohn day mehn
Voici la glace	Here's the ice cream	Vwa-see la glass (Glass with a short 'a', Northern English style)
Mais oui	But yes	May wee
C'est un verre	It's a glass	Set urn vair
Un verre de lait	A glass of milk	Earn vair de lay
C'est ça	That's it	Say sah (Short 'a' in ca, as in lass, not 'ay')
Et voici du pain	And here's some bread	Ay vwa-see doo pen
C'est un stylo	It's a pen	Set un steel-o
Un oeuf	An egg	Earn urff
Je comprends	I understand	Je comm-pron
Nous arrivons	We are here	Nooze arry von
Et voilà	And there	Ay vwa-lah
Au revoir	Goodbye (Till I see you again)	Oh re-vwa

2 FRANCE'S FOUR CORNERS

FRENCH	ENGLISH	PRONUNCIATION
Dordogne	Dordogne (French region)	Door-doyne
Lascaux	Lascaux (French village)	Lass-co
Les Eyzies	Les Eyzies (French village)	Laze-ay-see
Vézère	Vezere (French river)	Vez-air
Il s'appelle	He is called His name is	Il sap-ell

Je suis	I am	Je swee
Bonhomie	Good humour	Bonn-omm-ee
Superchic	Extra smart (We made it up!)	Soo-pair-sheek
Ooh là là!	Ooh, I say	Ooh la la

3   LET'S GO OVER

La classe	The litle darlings (The class)	La class (Short 'a' as in ass – as in donkey)
Madame	Married lady teacher	Mad-am
Comment ça va?	How are you? (Literally how goes it?)	Comm-on sa va
Acheter	To buy (verb) Buy! (command)	Ash-tay
Pâtisserie	Pastry shop	Pat-ees-eree
L'épicerie	Grocer's shop	Lay-pees-eree
Boulangerie	Bakery	Boo-long-jeree
Quel âge as tu?	How old are you?	Kell aj ah too
J'ai cinq ans	I am five (years old)	Jhay sank on
Mon ami a sept ans	My friend is seven	Mon amee a set on
Presque huit	Nearly eight	Press-quh wheat
Les saisons	The seasons	Lay say-zon
Il fait chaud	It's hot	Eel fay show
C'est l'été	It's summer	Say lay-tay
Il fait du vent	It's windy	Eel fay doo von
C'est l'automne	It's autumn	Say low-ton
Il neige	It's snowing	Eel nairje
C'est l'hiver	It's winter	Say lee-vair
Il pleut	It's raining	Eel plur
C'est le printemps	It's spring	Say le pran-tom
Qu'est-ce que c'est que ça?	What's that?	Kess kuh say kuh sa
Un arc-en-ciel	A rainbow (Literally an arch in the sky)	Earn ark-on-see-ell
Quelles couleurs vois-tu?	What colours do you see?	Kell koo-lur vwa-too
Rouge	Red	Rooj
Orange	Orange	O-ronge
Jaune	Yellow	Jawn
Vert	Green	Vair
Bleu	Blue	Bluh
Indigo	Indigo	An-dig-o (tricky, huh?)
Violet	Violet	Vee-oh-lay
Clair de lune	Moonlight	Clare de loon
Une pomme	An apple	Oon pomm
La terre	The ground	La tair
Pomme de terre	Potato	Pomm de tair
Zut!	Good grief!	Zoot!

Printed by
Halstan & Co. Ltd., Amersham, Bucks., England